What people are saying...

Andy Steiger is an unique voice among Christian Case Makers. He understands the culture, has a youthfully disarming approach, and is fearlessly passionate about sharing the Gospel. Best yet, Andy has been learning and refining his approach for years in coffee houses and other public settings. If you want to understand how to address life's most important issues so you can better respond to the culture's most pressing questions, Thinking is a must read.

J. Warner Wallace
Cold Case Detective
Author of Cold-Case Christianity and God's Crime Scene

This generation is searching for meaning in a variety of avenues and directions. Whether or not these individuals consider themselves to be thinkers, Andy Steiger's five biggest questions keep getting raised in an exceptionally wide variety of venues, from everyday coffee house chit-chat, to various media, to technical treatments. Addressing these subjects adequately can do more than just stimulate our minds. Finding the answers can lead us to absolutely exciting, fulfilling, and stimulating lives. To this end, I heartily recommend Steiger's book as a means of engaging in this quest for ultimate purpose and meaning.

Gary R. Habermas, Ph.D
Distinguished Research Professor & Chair, Dept. of Philosophy
Liberty University and Theological Seminary
Author of The Case for the Resurrection of Jesus

Andy Steiger has accomplished something very difficult in the modern world. He has written a tremendously engaging book that tackles the biggest questions that haunt every thoughtful person on the planet. And he has done it with great flair. I loved reading it and am anxious to give it to another dozen people who need to read it. It is a book that brings hope and light to everyone—from the believer to the hardcore skeptic. I hope churches and Bible study groups across North America sit down with this book and work through it. It would be hard to find a better way to grow in grace, truth, and joy.

Craig J. Hazen, Ph.D.
Founder and Director MA Program in Christian Apologetics
Biola University
Author of the novel *Five Sacred Crossings*

Andy Steiger has written a highly readable book that explores five of the most significant questions anyone could ask. Everyone thinks about these questions at one time or another but few are willing to discuss them openly, and even fewer people know where to turn for a thoughtful treatment of them. Steiger brings not only theoretical ideas to these questions but real heart as well. His many real-life illustrations will at times cause you to smile, at other times they will break your heart. Most importantly, they will help to illuminate the ideas under discussion and show how these concepts can be applied in real world situations.

Paul Chamberlain, Ph.D.
Director, Institute of Christian Apologetics
Associate Professor of Apologetics and Philosophy
Trinity Western University (ACTS Seminary)

THINKING?

Answering Life's Five Biggest Questions

THINKING?

Answering Life's Five Biggest Questions

ANDY STEIGER

with sheri hiebert

foreword by:
Sean McDowell

APOLOGETICS
CANADA

Thinking?

Published by Apologetics Canada Publishing
32040 Downes Road, Abbotsford, BC, V4X 1X5 Canada

Cover design and layout: Janine Boudreau
Author photo: Alyssa Schroeder Photography

Printed in Canada
First Edition 2015

ISBN: 978-0-99-401570-9
eISBN 978-0-9940157-1-6

*For my best friend Nancy and our deep thinkers,
Tristan and William.*

Acknowledgments

Thank you ...

Sheri Hiebert for all the sweat and tears you put into this project.

Nancy Steiger for making this book a reality.

Chris Battle for your friendship and your willingness to contribute your story to this book.

DJ Hiebert for encouraging me (Sheri) and listening patiently even though I talked about nothing but this book for the past six months.

Marj Hiebert for being a huge help to me (Sheri).

Steve Kim for keeping my writing neat and tidy.

Jeff Bucknam for pushing me deeper.

Kyle Meeker for not being afraid to make me rewrite sections.

Marj Drury for being a wonderful editor and encourager.

Angelika Obradovich, Jon Pasiuk, Jane Omelaniec, and Kelly Madland for helping make this a great book.

Northview Community Church for being a great church to grow and serve at.

Thinking Series Resources

Chapter Trailers:

Watch visually stunning and thought provoking videos introducing each question in this book.

What Is the Meaning of Life?
Have you ever wondered why you are here on this earth? We will explore what meaning is, where it's found, and if our life has any.

Does God Exist?
Is this universe and our life a meaningless accident? We will investigate who God is, the facts concerning His existence, and if He can be experienced.

Do All Religions Lead to God?
Can God be found within the maze of the world's religions? We will consider what other religions teach, if God can be found, and if God even wants to be reached.

Why Is There Evil?
Why is our world so full of poverty, violence and corruption? We will discuss what good and evil are, where they come from, and why they exist.

Is There Life After Death?
Have you ever wondered if this life is all there is? We will wrestle with what death is, why we die, and if God has done anything about it.

Think For a Minute videos:

For visual learners, these fast paced, engaging videos were designed to sketch out ideas from each chapter.

Available online at:
www.thinkingseries.com

Contents

Foreword by Sean McDowell xiii

Preface xv

Chapter One: What is the Meaning of Life? 1

Chapter Two: Does God Exist? 31

Chapter Three: Do All Religions Lead to God? 73

Chapter Four: Why is There Evil? 103

Chapter Five: Is There Life After Death? 137

Chapter Six: Becoming a Student 169

Notes 187

Reader's Guide 213

About the Coauthor 225

Foreword

These days, it is remarkably easy to find the answer to almost any question that pops into our minds. With just a few clicks on a keyboard, it takes us only seconds to access more facts, opinions, and depths of knowledge than previous generations could only hope to learn in a lifetime. It is so easy to get lost in all the information. We can find ourselves heading down the rabbit-trails of Wikipedia, exploring questions we didn't even know we had, about topics we once had no interest in.

So, in a culture like ours, filled to bursting with data, you might assume that there are no more questions left that are worth asking. Yet, such an assumption couldn't be more mistaken. Despite living in the Information Age, our culture is impoverished when it comes to providing thoughtful answers to the most important questions of life. *Why are we here? Is there a God? Why do we suffer? What happens next?* These are the questions that our culture desperately needs answers for.

That's why I'm thrilled that you are holding these pages in your hands. *Thinking?: Answering Life's Five Biggest Questions* is a timely book. It answers life's biggest questions with refreshing honesty, clarity, passion, and depth. Andy is a natural storyteller with a gift for unwrapping complicated ideas without the insider jargon and fifty-dollar words that only bring confusion. If you think that philosophy, history, and theology are as dry as sawdust, then this book will startle you with its relevance and poignancy. Andy's stories will not only have you laughing and crying, but will get you thinking and inspire you to focus on what's most important: loving God and other people (Mark 12:30-31).

I'm thankful to Apologetics Canada for providing this commendable book at a time when our culture needs it the most. My prayer is that it will equip you to make a difference for the Kingdom of God in a generation that so desperately needs both grace and truth.

Sincerely,
Sean McDowell, Ph.D.
Biola University Professor, Speaker,
and Co-author of *Is God Just A Human Invention?*

Preface

In 2010, I was approached by Velocity, a Christian organization that holds music concerts, comedy shows, and lectures in a coffee shop in Port Moody, British Columbia. They were wondering if I would be willing to give a series of lectures on life's five biggest questions from a Christian perspective. "Sure," I said.

But there was a hitch. They suggested doing something that they had never done before: they wanted to hold the lectures during normal operating hours. Velocity normally rented the coffee shop, closing it to the public for their events. This time, however, they wanted to keep the store open, allowing people to come and go freely, while I spoke in the corner.

I must confess, I was a little concerned about this idea. My mind filled with visions of hostile baristas and annoyed customers throwing their empty cups at the crazy guy giving a lecture to no one. Although I was a little terrified, I was also excited to give it a try.

With a little research and a lot of common sense, I came up with the list of life's five biggest questions:

1) What is the meaning of life?
2) Does God exist?
3) Do all religions lead to God?
4) Why is there evil?
5) Is there life after death?

We spent a couple of weeks promoting the lecture series and then it was time for the main event. When I arrived at Gallagher's Coffee Bar and Cafe that first evening for "The Big Five," as we called it back then, the coffee shop was dead quiet.

Would anybody even show up?

We began to arrange chairs and a local musician started prepping his sound equipment. Slowly, people started trickling in. Then, as the musician played, the coffeeshop began to fill with people that had come for the talk. I was blown away by the response! What I thought would be a handful of cantankerous coffee addicts, turned into over sixty-five excited people jammed into a small space. There were all kinds of thinkers and perspectives represented including Atheist, Agnostic, New Age, and Christian. By the time I began, it was standing room only. While I spoke on the meaning of life, you could hear the espresso machine humming, the cash register slamming, and the sound of people sipping coffee. It was glorious!

During my talk, I noticed quite a few random people coming into the coffee shop off of the street and—to my surprise—they were staying. I even noticed that people who were walking their dogs or just going for a stroll were stopping outside the door and listening. 'What were these people thinking?', I wondered, 'did they think I was crazy?!' After spending the first half of our time together raising the question of life's meaning, I took a break to allow time for people to discuss the question with those around them. As the aroma of freshly brewed coffee filled the air, so did the conversation.

The coffee shop was abuzz with excitement. As I sat at different tables, listening to the ideas people were discussing, I could sense that many people had a deep longing to be heard and to discuss this profound question. People continued to come in off the street and join in to the conversation.

With the time remaining, I did my best to address the question in a way that was personal, passionate, and understandable. Ultimately, I just wanted to get people thinking about important questions of life; too often, our culture has made these questions seem unanswerable. I think that's why the series was such a hit; there are just not many places you can go to these days to have meaningful conversation about the big issues of life.

The night went so well that the owner of Gallagher's literally needed to push people out of his shop so that he could close up for the night. Eagerly, he invited us to come back for the next topic. Over the next five weeks, we continued to pack it out. The owner made a tidy profit, and I learned a lot. Since then, I have given hundreds of lectures on each of these topics in coffee shops, bars, universities, high schools, conferences, and churches. Eventually, these talks led to the creation of a DVD and this book, that together are called the *Thinking Series*. This series is designed to help the church engage with a culture that is desperate for answers. The *Thinking Series* is also an online course that can be taken for college credit, a certificate, or just for fun.

This series is the result of years of conversations and research on these topics. You'll see that life's five biggest questions are all interconnected and, when put together, they help to clearly explain why Jesus is good news. So, whether you are new to these types of discussions, or an old pro, I hope this book helps expose you to new ideas and thinkers, as well as encourage you as you wrestle through these important questions with others.

For more information on the Thinking Series, the online course, or to host your own discussions, please visit: www.thinkingseries.com.

Chapter One

What is the Meaning of Life?

The day after I graduated from college, I boarded a plane bound for Kathmandu, Nepal. Ever since I was a young boy, I had dreamed of hiking the Himalayas and getting a glimpse of the world's tallest mountain. I had hoped to make the hike to Mount Everest with a good friend of mine, but at the last minute, his girlfriend told him that she would break up with him if he went, so I ended up making the journey alone. Ironically, after arriving in Nepal, he emailed me to say that she had broken up with him anyway. Served him right.

For three weeks, I teahouse-trekked through the Himalayas with a middle-aged Sherpa named Sung, whom I had hired to guide me to Mount Everest base camp.[1] Sung led me through the valleys and passes, keeping me on the right trail and identifying the mountain peaks along the way. I hiked past five of the world's tallest mountains; they rose up one after the other, stunning against a backdrop of dark blue sky and cirrus clouds. These peaks were truly majestic and foreboding. Often, I would pass long caravans of yaks loaded with gear and food for upcoming expeditions.

Eventually, we reached Mount Everest base camp. Sung, who was a well-known Sherpa and had set ropes on Everest many times before, introduced me to other Sherpas and western climbers who were there to attempt a summit of the famous peak. Many of these teams had been there for months: acclimatizing, setting ropes, and making camps for their ascent. I remember talking with one businessman from Los Angeles who wanted desperately to reach the summit. A picture of himself atop this exclusive rock was a trophy he was willing to pay and risk everything for. It was clear from our conversation that he was not there for the joy of mountaineering, but simply to add this prestigious summit to his list of accomplishments.

My experience at base camp left me perplexed: why would people put themselves through so much, even risk their very lives, just for a chance to climb a mountain? Yet, as I descended the Himalayas on my return to Kathmandu, I began to realize that I wasn't so different.

The Career Caste System

I grew up in a poor and broken family. My parents separated when I was four years old, leaving my mother to raise four children on her own. We moved from Redding, California, to Portland, Oregon, with nothing and started over. My mom worked hard at a bank to care for us all. She did everything in her power to give us a chance at life. In many ways, my mom sacrificed her dreams and desires for the sake of her children. Perhaps that's why I've never forgotten the way she would pull me aside while I was growing up, and say, "Andy. I know you will do great things with your life."

I knew my mom meant those words to encourage me, but instead they became a burden! When you're a kid, doing great things is fairly easy, like graduating from diapers or learning to ride a bike. However, the older I got, the more complicated it became. The truth is: I didn't want to disappoint my mom, but at the same time, I had no idea how to accomplish "great things."

I mean, what exactly qualifies?

I think we all have that sense deep within us for something more. We all want to make something of our lives, but we're not sure exactly how. Ultimately, these desires left me frustrated and anxious. While I was in high school, I had very little self-esteem and almost no drive to do anything with my life. I had just given up. Life was quickly becoming meaningless. Eventually, this attitude led me to peers with a similar outlook. It didn't take long until we began to seek answers with alcohol and drugs - yet, the highs never lasted. Naturally, we felt a push towards harder alcohol and drugs, in an attempt to achieve what the previous high could not. One day, as I was offered some harder drugs, I clearly saw that I had arrived at a crossroads; I needed to choose which direction my life would go. Saint Augustine (AD 354-430), a renowned Christian thinker writing in the fourth century, said that the heart of man is restless.[2] That was exactly how I felt. I was restless. I didn't know the answer that I was seeking, but I knew where it couldn't be found. That day I gave up on alcohol and drugs.

However, what I was really doing was just swapping one high for another.

Unsure of how to satisfy my restlessness without alcohol and drugs, I instead followed culture. Without really thinking about it, I began to occupy my restless energy with a life of accomplishment climbing. Looking back, it's now obvious to me how I arrived on that path. Have you ever noticed how Western culture defines people by their accomplishments? After all, what are the first two questions we ask people when we meet them for the first time? "What's your name?" and "What do you do for a living?" The answers to those questions tell us everything that we need to know in order to judge their success, and ultimately their worth, by Western standards. We may call it "climbing the corporate ladder," but it's really a career caste system; some careers are at the top and some are at the bottom, and nobody is confused about which is which. I mean, where does a Supreme Court judge rank? How about a surgeon? Or a gas station attendant? You get my point. Dress your profession up with a technical name, but at the end of the day, who are we really fooling? If we're honest with ourselves, we are all guilty of placing others and ourselves in the career caste system.

So, what's the alternative?

If your name and profession don't define you, what should?

When I graduated from high school, I found myself overwhelmed by all of the different types of accomplishments I could pursue. I decided to start by tackling college. Considering that no one in my family had ever earned a degree, this seemed like a good place to begin an assault on "great things." It wasn't long until I had a good list of achievements under my belt: I graduated from college, hiked to Mount Everest, got married, traveled the world, bought a house, had kids, completed a Master's degree, and founded an organization.

For a while, accomplishment climbing worked; I found that reaching the summit of my goals was exhilarating! Standing on top of my accomplishments provided me a brief high, a flash of relief, and for a moment, my restless heart was calmed. I felt on top of the world, with the view of my accomplishments stretched out beneath me. In those moments, I wanted to yell out: "This is it! I've made it! This is what I live for!" Yet, it never lasted. Soon the moment would pass, my restlessness would come flooding back, and I would descend another of life's peaks frustrated.

Valley Floor

You see, what is true of mountain ranges is also true of life: you can't have mountains unless you have valleys. Accomplishment climbing, or pleasure seeking through drugs, alcohol, and sex, ensures that we will have low times of restlessness and despair. It's in these valleys where we begin to fix our attention on the next summit, setting our sights continually higher in hopes that the next high will achieve what the previous couldn't. So begins a never-ending cycle, a progression of peaks and valleys, with the peaks growing ever higher and the valleys sinking ever deeper. It shouldn't surprise us when so many people struggle with a midlife crisis or hit rock bottom; with each new peak comes an equally difficult valley, until eventually the valley becomes so deep you just can't get out of it anymore. Before we set our sights too high and descend too low, we can learn from those that have climbed higher achievements than us.

One of my favorite comedians is Jim Carrey. He's funny, wealthy, and famous. Yet, in a 2014 commencement speech, he said, "I've often said that I wished people could realize all their dreams of wealth and fame, so they could see that it's not where you'll find your sense of completion."[3] This is exactly what King Solomon experienced. Solomon was the King of Israel from around 970-931 BC and he was renowned for having everything; he was intelligent, wealthy, and powerful, yet none of that satisfied him. In his book *Ecclesiastes*, which is found in the Bible, he wrote:

> I said to myself, "Come on, let's try pleasure. Let's look for the 'good things' in life." But I found that this, too, was meaningless. So I said, "Laughter is silly. What good does it do to seek pleasure?" After much thought, I decided to cheer myself with wine. And while still seeking wisdom, I clutched at foolishness. In this way, I tried to experience the only happiness most people find during their brief life in this world. I also tried to find meaning by building huge homes for myself and by planting beautiful vineyards. I made gardens and parks, filling them with all kinds of fruit trees. I built reservoirs to collect the water to irrigate my many flourishing groves. I bought slaves, both men and women, and others were born into my household. I also owned large herds and flocks, more than any of the kings who had lived in Jerusalem before me. I collected great sums of silver and gold, the treasure of many kings and provinces. I hired wonderful singers, both men and women, and had many beautiful

concubines. I had everything a man could desire! So I became greater than all who had lived in Jerusalem before me, and my wisdom never failed me. Anything I wanted, I would take. I denied myself no pleasure. I even found great pleasure in hard work, a reward for all my labors. But as I looked at everything I had worked so hard to accomplish, it was all so meaningless—like chasing the wind. There was nothing really worthwhile anywhere.[4]

In today's culture, we don't usually envy kings like Solomon. Instead, we envy people like Tom Brady. He is arguably the greatest quarterback of all time; he's wealthy, athletic, and has a supermodel for a wife. Yet, in a TV interview for 60 *Minutes*, he said, "Why do I have three Super Bowl rings and still think there's something greater out there for me? I mean, maybe a lot of people would say, 'Hey man, this is what it is.' I reached my goal, my dream, my life. Me, I think, 'God, it's got to be more than this.'" Steve Kroft quickly asked, "What's the answer?" Tom responded, "I wish I knew. I wish I knew."[5]

At some level, don't statements like these shock us? It's difficult to believe that the accomplishments we think would surely satisfy us didn't satisfy them! Yet, that's because there truly is no top, no ultimate peak that will satisfy. Instead, there are only varying levels of success, with all of us jostling for position. Even those who have climbed Everest experience this. Sure it's the tallest mountain, but: Which route did you take? What support did you have? Did you do it with oxygen tanks? How many times have you summited? It's not surprising that our accomplishments never satisfy. How can they? That's the problem with wealth, success, and greatness: there's always more wealth to acquire, more to succeed at, and there will always be someone greater than you.

The news is full of celebrities who testify to this through their addictions, obsessions, and depression. They're a constant reminder that it's never enough. Sex, drugs, and accomplishments will never satisfy you. Sadly, it's a cycle that has led many people to give up on life and even commit suicide.

Avoiding Suicide

This was almost the case for Leo Tolstoy (1828-1910), a famous Russian novelist. (He wrote *War and Peace* and *Anna Karenina*, amongst many other works.) In his book, *A Confession*, an autobiographical journey into his midlife crisis, Tolstoy explains that from all indications he should have been a happy man. He wasn't yet fifty, he had a good and loving wife, great kids, a large house, and fame. Yet, he writes, "And in such a state of affairs I came to a point where I could not live; and even though I feared death, I had to employ ruses against myself to keep from committing suicide."[6]

The restlessness of accomplishment climbing brought him to pen these words:

> I could not attach a rational meaning to a single act in my entire life. The only thing that amazed me was how I had failed to realize this in the very beginning. All this had been common knowledge for so long. If not today, then tomorrow sickness and death will come (indeed, they were already approaching) to everyone, to me, and nothing will remain except the stench and the worms. My deeds, whatever they may be, will be forgotten sooner or later, and I myself will be no more. Why then do anything? How can anyone fail to see this and live? That's what is amazing! It is possible to live only as long as life intoxicates us; once we are sober

we cannot help seeing that it is all a delusion, a stupid delusion! Nor is there anything funny or witty about it; it is only cruel and stupid.[7]

Tolstoy didn't take his life, but he did begin to look outside of his accomplishments to satisfy his restless heart. Have you ever considered that if we are unable to quench the restlessness within us it's because we were made for something far greater than we can satisfy?[8] Christian thinker C.S. Lewis (1898-1963) put it this way:

> Creatures are not born with desires unless satisfaction for those desires exists. A baby feels hunger: well, there is such a thing as food. A duckling wants to swim: well, there is such a thing as water. Men feel sexual desire: well, there is such a thing as sex. If I find in myself a desire which no experience in this world can satisfy, the most probable explanation is that I was made for another world.[9]

Lewis isn't saying that every one of our desires will be satisfied; people die of hunger and thirst every day. Rather, what he's saying is that we, as humans, never have an innate desire for something that does not exist or is incapable of being filled.[10]

So, what does that say about our desire for meaning?

If humans universally have a desire for meaning and value in life, doesn't that suggest that meaning actually exists?

This challenge caused me to take a step back from culture and begin a new journey to answer one of life's big questions: what is the meaning of life?

What is Meaning?

When we say that something has meaning, we are referring to more than just the existence of something. Rather, meaning comes when someone with the power to do so, such as an author or creator, *gives* meaning to something. For example, think of a musician. When a composer takes musical notes, which are just mechanical waves of pressure which the human brain interprets as specific sounds, and strings them together with purpose, in such a way as to invoke a certain emotion, and adds lyrics that convey the musician's heart, everyone recognizes that meaning has been created. What started as merely sound becomes music when it is infused with meaning. As artists, composers, and authors, that's what we do; we endow the objects of our creation with information, significance, purpose, and worth. Only then can something be said to have meaning. The philosopher Dr. Thomas V. Morris agrees and says, "It follows from this that in any sense of the word 'meaning,' if anything in my life is to havemeaning (or a meaning), it must be endowed with meaning. It must be *given* meaning. Meaning is never intrinsic; it is always derivative."[11]

Meaning has to be *given* to something—it must come from an author.[12]

Decoding a Mystery

Sometimes, we can know something has meaning, but it can be difficult to tell what that meaning is. Allow me to illustrate this point with an example from a once-dead language—Egyptian Hieroglyphics. Prior to 1822, the markings that cover the ancient structures and artifacts of Egypt were a complete mystery. It was obvious that the ancient Egyptians had given the markings meaning, and that together they made up a language, but the meaning had been lost to time. Scholars made a variety of guesses, but no amount of study could truly decipher them. The ancient language of the Egyptians was dead, because the meaning had been lost.

This began to change in 1799, when a now-famous rock was discovered near Alexandria, Egypt, in the town of Rosetta (Rashid). This granite-type stone would come to be called the Rosetta Stone and on it was written the same message in three scripts: Egyptian Hieroglyphics, Demotic, and ancient Greek. It took over twenty years, but using the meaning from Greek and other languages, scholars were able to rediscover the meaning of Egyptian Hieroglyphics. The once-dead language suddenly came alive again! If you have ever studied a foreign language, computer code, or texting acronyms, you know what it's like for strange markings, symbols, and letter combinations to come alive once their meaning is explained to you. This is exactly what the Rosetta Stone accomplished.

What if the same is true of life? Could human life be like a dead language containing a treasure of knowledge, significance, worth, and purpose, just waiting to be rediscovered? Is this why we are restless? We keep trying to read a dead language but nothing makes sense. We sense that our lives have meaning, but we just can't access it.

The Bare Necessities

Now, you might be wondering: can't we just give our own lives meaning? That's a good question because it draws attention to the two forms of meaning: subjective and objective. Subjective meaning is the personal significance we give to other people's work; it is subject—to you. Thus, this type of meaning changes from person to person. The love song I first danced to with my wife is full of meaning for me—but it's subjective meaning. On the other hand, objective meaning is the meaning we give to the things we create or control. Because it is based on the intent of the author, objective meaning will remain the same for everyone. For example, the composer of that same love song could tell me the reason he wrote it and that would be the objective meaning.

Consider, that before 1822, a person could have studied Egyptian Hieroglyphics and ascribed whatever meaning they wanted to the symbols. But would that meaning have been the true meaning? Of course not! That meaning would have been subjective. In order to actually read the language, we needed to know the objective meaning, the intended meaning given it by its authors, in this case the Ancient Egyptians.

This distinction was made clear to me personally one day when I came home from work. I found one of my son's "hieroglyphic" stick figure drawings taped to his bedroom door. It contained four figures—two large and two small. The two large stick figures were circled with a line through them. "That doesn't look good," I thought to myself. Now, I could have taken an educated guess at what the picture meant, but I might have been wrong. Likewise, I could have given it personal significance, but I would still be no closer to understanding its intended meaning. To discover the intended meaning of anything, you need to somehow access the author that created it. In this case, it was easy: I asked my son. After a few questions, I learned that the drawing meant Mom and Dad were not allowed to come into his room during wrestling matches with his younger brother. In other words, he didn't want us to stop him from beating up his younger brother. Well, that wasn't going to happen!

Just as objective meaning was necessary in order to understand Hieroglyphics or my son's drawing, objective meaning is necessary in order to decipher the meaning of life. Subjective meaning is just not capable of answering the questions "why am I here?" and "what meaning was I created for?" Answering those foundational questions requires objective meaning, found only in the creator of life—God.

It's easy to misunderstand this last point, so allow me to clarify what I'm *not* saying. I'm not saying that you need to believe in God in order to live a subjectively meaningful life. I believe that people can give their lives personal meaning and significance without appealing to God. In fact, we do it all the time! I have a love for hiking, and this passion does contribute to the meaning of my life, but what I'm talking about is much more basic. I want to know why I exist. The truth is, we did not bring ourselves into existence. Thus, it is beyond our control to give the whole of human life, or our own life in particular, objective meaning. Morris explains this well when he says:

> So what exactly is outside the scope of our control? Well, to put it bluntly, nothing more than birth, life, suffering, and death. And if all this is outside our control, we do not have the requisite control to see to it that our lives are completely meaningful, through and through, from first to last. We can create islands of meaning in this sea of existence we've been given, but...it seems that anything we build we will build with materials that have been given to us.[13]

This is why a search for the meaning of life inevitably leads to questions about the existence of God. Yet, before we talk about God, one more thing is necessary in order for life to have lasting objective meaning: eternal life.

Forever and Ever

Let's turn once more to the example of Egyptian Hieroglyphics. In that case, the markings existed, but the meaning of them had been lost. What if the markings themselves had been lost, the way they have been for countless languages in the past? It's obvious that the meaning would also be lost. In the same way, when we die, any meaning that was given to our life, or that we gave it, dies with us. How meaningful is life if it is just destroyed in the end? If life is temporal, then so is our meaning.

A college student once challenged me on this point, asking, "But what if I left a legacy after I die? Wouldn't that give my life enduring meaning?" I understood what she was getting at. Can my life have meaning that outlives me because people will remember me? Well, so far Egyptian Hieroglyphics have lasted almost five thousand years and that's pretty impressive. However, no matter how well preserved, it will be forgotten sooner or later. It reminds me of the famous poem, *Ozymandias*, in which Percy Bysshe Shelley (1792-1822) captures the problem:

> I met a traveller from an antique land
> Who said: Two vast and trunkless legs of stone
> Stand in the desert... Near them, on the sand,
> Half sunk, a shattered visage lies, whose frown,
> And wrinkled lip, and sneer of cold command,
> Tell that its sculptor well those passions read
> Which yet survive, stamped on these lifeless things,
> The hand that mocked them, and the heart that fed:
> And on the pedestal these words appear:
> 'My name is Ozymandias, king of kings:

Look on my works, ye Mighty, and despair!'
Nothing beside remains. Round the decay
Of that colossal wreck, boundless and bare
The lone and level sands stretch far away.[14]

In the poem, Ozymandias was the most powerful of rulers and thought that his legacy would last forever. Yet, in the end, it all became sand. Ozymandias is shown to be nothing but a fool and his statue, rather than boasting of his works, speaks only of his ruin. Likewise, your accomplishments, no matter how great, will be lost to time eventually. Worse than that, physics tells us that as our sun dies it will continue to grow until it engulfs the earth in fire, removing any trace that you ever existed. Humanity's extinction is unavoidable. Even if we were able to move to other planets, humanity won't outlive the universe. Again, physics' diagnosis for our universe is terminal! The second law of thermodynamics reminds us that the heat death of the universe is taking place and, eventually, nothing will remain but a cold lifeless universe in ruins. This brings us back to Tolstoy's dilemma: if life is *ultimately* going to end in ruin what real meaning does it have? In the weight of eternity, why bother doing anything?

This has left some people to wonder, what if people didn't die and somehow we were able to live forever? Would that provide our lives with meaning? No, by itself eternal life alone can't provide meaning. In fact, the Greek myth of Sisyphus illustrates how eternity alone can actually turn life into utter hopelessness. The story goes like this: Sisyphus was a king condemned by Zeus for his trickery. Sisyphus' punishment was to roll a massive boulder to the top of a steep hill. However, every time he got the boulder near the top of the hill, it would roll back down to the bottom, making him start over and over again, for all eternity. For Sisyphus, the task was meaningless in and of itself, but it became utterly hopeless when he could never actually complete it. The end of all things, or annihilation, would have been preferred.

The point is that infinite duration alone doesn't provide meaning to an otherwise meaningless life. Although you may have a vessel, even a potentially eternal one, it does not follow that it would suddenly fill with meaning. Increasing the duration of a meaningless life does not change what it is—meaningless. For us mortals, death is a constant reminder of our need and desire for meaning; yet, if we were eternal, what death's nagging could not achieve, boredom and hopelessness would. In fact, I think it would make things worse! At least temporary meaninglessness would eventually come to an end, but eternal meaninglessness would be unbearable. However, if eternal life is possible, then we are back once again to the search for objective meaning.

Life's Author

By now it should be clear that in order for something to have true meaning it needs to have been given it by the person who authored or created it. Since people did not bring themselves into existence, we can't be our own author. Instead, we need someone who created the universe and human life in particular— we need someone like God. Simply put: if God exists, life has objective meaning, and if God does not exist, human life is a meaningless cosmic accident.

Ever since the Enlightenment, it has been the intention of humanity to explain the natural world through natural causes alone. Yet, this naturalistic worldview carries implications that the German philosopher, Friedrich Nietzsche (1844-1900), pointed out and explained. In his book, *The Gay Science*, Nietzsche illustrated his insights with a parable entitled "The Madman."[15] In this story, a madman runs into the village shouting, "I seek God! I seek God!" The man is mocked and ridiculed by the townspeople who, not believing in God, shout back, "Is God hiding? Did He go on a voyage?" In response to their scornful reply, the Madman runs into the crowd and cries out:

> [Where] is God? I shall tell you. *We have killed him*—you and I. All of us are his murderers. But how have we done this?...What did we do when we unchained this earth from its sun?...Are we not plunging continually? Backward, sideward, forward, in all directions? Is there any up or down left? Are we not straying as through an infinite nothing? Do we not feel the breath of empty space?...God is dead...And we have killed him. How shall we, the murderers of all murderers, comfort ourselves?[16]

At the end of the story, the Madman realizes that the atheistic townspeople don't yet understand the implications of God's death. They're ignorant of the ramifications of life that has no author. In fact, Nietzsche wrote this story, not for those that believe in God, but rather for those who, like himself, did not. He believed it was those who had "buried" God, both culturally and personally, that didn't understand the implications of that funeral.

Nietzsche understood that an author, God, provided the foundation and structural support from which a person or culture can find objective meaning. By the "death of God," Nietzsche was saying that the foundation had collapsed; the meaning of life could no longer be supported. Without God, we can't even tell up from down.

As Nietzsche puts it in the quotation above, now that we are "unchained" from a divine worldview, we are lost, floating through a cold, dark, hopeless universe. What the Enlightenment illuminated was a meaningless universe into which humans peered and gasped at its implications. If the physical world came from nothing and will return to nothing, it is painfully obvious that we are in fact—nothing. As Philosopher and Theologian William Lane Craig explains: "Nietzsche predicted that someday people would realize the implications of their atheism; and this realization would usher in an age of nihilism—the destruction of all meaning and value in life."[17]

A Conversation with Greenpeace

Interestingly, although this is the implication of many people's worldview, they do not in fact live as though this is true. I once explained this to a person promoting Greenpeace. Stepping out of a bookstore in downtown Portland, I was greeted by a friendly advocate. The man had a clipboard and was wearing a t-shirt with "GREENPEACE" across the front. As I walked past, he asked if he could talk with me. I said, "Sure." The young man was delighted and began eagerly promoting the environment, explaining how important the earth is, and how we need to care for it. After he presented some dramatic stories and disheartening statistics, I said, "Can I ask you a question?" He said, "Yes." With genuine interest, I asked, "Why do you care about the environment?" To my surprise, the man said nothing. He stared at me blankly, completely stumped.

Considering that he was on the street promoting the environment, I found his hesitation a little ironic. After some time of reflection, he said, "I guess to take care of it for future generations." "That's interesting," I said, "Can I ask you another question?" Although he said "Yes," I could tell he wasn't completely sure he wanted another question. I asked, "Do you believe in God?" Now at this point, I'm sure he was thinking, 'I shouldn't have stopped this guy. *This* is the guy I should have let keep walking.' However, he graciously pondered my question and, after a long pause said, "I'm not sure."

"Well, here's what I'm thinking," I said, "If God doesn't exist, it means this world is just the product of physical forces and doesn't have any real meaning or value. If anything, I should just use what I can from the earth before the sun gobbles it up." With a look of shock and disgust he blurted out, "Dude that's messed up!" (Actually, what he really said was more like "Dude that's $%#@&^ up!") "I know! I know!" I said, "I actually think the earth *does* have value and we *should* take care of it, but it's because it has an author." This young man suddenly became very interested in the way I explained my passion for the environment, because it validated his.

He and I had something in common: we both desired to protect and care for a masterpiece. I suggested to this man from Greenpeace that the earth should be cared for and his efforts were important because this earth is a priceless work of art, endowed with meaning by a powerful author–God. Imagine, however, if this rock we call earth is authorless, a speck of dust in the vastness of space, destined to be engulfed by a dying star we affectionately call the sun. It raises the question: why care what happens to a meaningless space rock?

What's true of this planet is also true of people. If people have no author and are merely awaiting inescapable destruction, why fight to protect meaningless lives? People might as well just live to get what they can, while they can. Yes, it might be mutually beneficial, even rational to care for the environment and people, but why bother? It would be like painting a house that's in the path of a tornado.

Certainly, taking care of the environment is beneficial because it provides me with clean water, and caring for people creates a better world for us to live in. This would be rational behavior; yet, the Nihilist's question is: Why be rational? On what grounds can selflessness or charity be praised? In the end, none of it really matters. If people are merely the result of natural processes, then Nietzsche is right—we have no ultimate meaning, purpose, or value. Humanity is just a short blip of time in a pointless universe. It's all quite depressing, really. A world without meaning is like a black hole into which everything, even our very passion for living, is inescapably sucked.

What is the Meaning of Life?

Once again, if we want to know the meaning of life we first need to determine if there is an author of life and if eternal life is possible. Those are two huge questions! Further, even if we answer both of those questions positively, a third question is raised: if life *does* have an author and eternal life *is* possible, which world religion can properly explain that author's intentions? The fact is, talking about the meaning of life raises so many additional questions that in order to talk about it at all, we are going to have to make some major assumptions and then address them later. So, where to start?

We need to start somewhere. There are four reasons why I believe that any search for the meaning of life should begin with Jesus Christ. First, Jesus claimed to be the author of life. This is a unique claim. Most religious leaders claim to hear from God, but Jesus spoke with his own authority, claiming to be

God in the flesh. Second, Jesus satisfies all of the necessities we discussed earlier; he not only claimed to be the author of life, but he also taught that eternal life is possible through him. Third, Jesus' answer is testable; we can see if it really does make sense of our experience in life. Fourth, nearly all other religions venerate Jesus in some way: for the Jews he was a rabbi, for the Muslims a prophet, and for the Buddhist a moral teacher. So, if the task of answering the meaning of life is to hear from the author of life, it just makes sense to start with Jesus. Now, I appreciate that I am making some major assumptions in doing so. For instance, I am assuming that God exists, that Jesus is who he claimed to be, and that eternal life is possible, but my purpose in introducing you right away to Jesus' answer is so that you can spend the rest of the book seeing if it's true. We will address the assumptions and questions surrounding them in the remaining chapters of the book.

Jesus' Answer

Jesus' teaching on the meaning of life can be clearly seen in two dialogues found in the Bible: both in Mark 12. The first is a famous dialogue about paying taxes (of all things)! Jesus had just returned to Jerusalem after having raised a ruckus. He was frustrated with how people were using religion for their own gain and he ended up telling off a bunch of people in the temple. Now, the religious leaders were frustrated with Jesus and wanted to trap him in his words in front of his followers in order to diminish his influence—maybe even get him arrested. They asked Jesus two simple, but loaded, questions: "Is it right to pay taxes to Caesar or not? Should we pay or shouldn't we?"

This was a great set up given the context! In the first century, the Jews were completely controlled by Rome. As a conquered people, they were mistreated and forced to pay taxes to Rome. If Jesus responds that the Jews, who want their freedom from the Romans, must pay the unpopular tax to an oppressive foreign government, then his followers are going to be angry and leave him. However, if Jesus instructs them *not* to pay the tax, the Roman authorities will be angry and Jesus could be arrested. Fully aware of their trap, Jesus asks for a denarius, a coin that was used to pay the tax. They hand him the coin and Jesus holds it up for all to see. He asks, "Whose portrait is this? And whose inscription?" "Caesar's," they replied. Then Jesus said to them, "Give to Caesar what is Caesar's and to God what is God's."[18]

The Bible records that those listening were amazed at his answer! What was so profound about it? It's not what Jesus said, but what he *implied*. The first is obvious: give to Caesar what belongs to Caesar—the coin; Jesus is telling the people to pay their taxes. The second implication is not as obvious to us in the twenty-first century, but to a first century Jew, it was powerfully clear. When Jesus said to give to God what *is* God's, it raised the question: "What is God's?" Well, just like the coin belonged to Caesar because it bore his image, so that which bears God's image belongs to God. The Jews understood that *people* bear the image of God! In Genesis 1:27, it says, "So God created man in his own image, in the image of God he created him; male and female he created them."

Jesus took their question and did more than address taxes. Instead, he challenged them to give to God what belongs to him—their very lives—and to live for the purpose they were created for.

Relationally Made

A little farther into Mark 12, we are told that those listening to Jesus were impressed by his answers, so they decided to press him. An expert in Jewish law asked Jesus: "Of all the commandments, which is the most important?" This is the Jewish equivalent of asking, "What's the meaning or purpose of life? What's the most important thing to know?" "The most important one," answered Jesus, "is this: Hear, O Israel, the Lord our God, the Lord is one."

Basically, Jesus starts by reminding them that life has only one author—God. He then said these famous words: "Love the Lord your God with all your heart and with all your soul and with all your mind and with all your strength. The second is this: Love your neighbor as yourself. There is no commandment greater than these."[19]

The meaning of life, defined by Jesus, is simple—love God. The message of the Bible from beginning to end repeats this same message: God loves you and created you for relationship. You were created to know and be known, to love and be loved. In fact, those listening would instantly have recognized that Jesus is quoting the *Shema*, a prayer that occurs in Deuteronomy 6:4-9:

> Hear, O Israel: The Lord our God, the Lord is one. Love the Lord your God with all your heart and with all your soul and with all your strength. These commandments that I give you today are to be upon your hearts. Impress them on your children. Talk about them when you sit at home and when you walk along the road, when you lie down and when you get up. Tie them as symbols on your hands and bind them on your foreheads. Write them on the doorframes of your houses and on your gates.

The Bible teaches that our need for relationship is much deeper than we can fully appreciate. Reflect back on Jesus' first challenge—that we were created in the image of God. The Bible teaches that God is a Trinity, one God in three persons: Father, Son, and Holy Spirit. He embodies relationship within his very being. Accordingly, we were created in the image of a relational God. We all have a deep desire for relationship that no drug, achievement, or human relationship can fully satisfy. We were created for relationship with God.

However, if you noticed, Jesus added something to the *Shema* at the end, a summary of Leviticus 19 in which God explains to Moses how his people are to treat one another. He starts by saying, "Be holy because I, the Lord your God, am holy."[20] Then, God explains to Moses what holiness looks like in our relationships, summarizing it all saying, "Do not seek revenge or bear a grudge against a fellow Israelite, but love your neighbor as yourself. I am the Lord."[21] Jesus consistently taught that your love for God and his love for you will inspire you to become more like him—holy—and that this will lead you to show love for other people. In fact, Jesus taught that people will know you belong to him if you love one another.[22] However, we need to get the order right. First and foremost, we were created to love God because God first loved us.[23] It's from our relationship with God that we learn to love one another.

Jesus was a living demonstration of the lengths that God would go to make his love known. The Bible explains that Jesus is the author of life—God in the flesh. Instead of revealing himself as a far-off idea or cosmic guru, God willingly left heaven and came to earth as a baby to make himself known in a way that we could understand—as a human being. It's hard to express the scandal of that: the one who is greater than everything in existence, became close enough for us to touch, near enough to be seen sweating, weeping, and bleeding.[24]

The vast majority of the Bible is narrative; it's the story of God and his people. At the beginning, we were in a right and loving relationship with God, but then we willingly rejected him and severed the relationship. God, however, did not give up on his people, sending his son Jesus as a servant in order to bring us back into relationship with himself.

Still Restless?

Remember that restlessness we were talking about earlier? Saint Augustine went on to say, "You have made us for yourself, and our heart is restless until it rests in you."[25] We were made to live in relationship with God. Jesus' answer to the meaning of life changed my life because it changed my focus. I stopped trying to restlessly make an image for myself and started resting in the one in whose image I was made. In Jesus, I have inherited true wealth, success, and a legacy that never ends—relationship with God. I no longer look to people or my accomplishments to satisfy me—they can't. I am satisfied by living for God's glory rather than my own. This doesn't mean that the peaks and valleys of life are gone; in many ways my relationship with God has encouraged me to climb even higher. I just stopped trying to find my meaning in it. We don't need to go through the peaks and valleys of life alone; we were meant to experience all of life together in relationship with God.

Conclusion

I am convinced that most people intuitively know that life is about more than accomplishment climbing or pleasure seeking. It just requires that they take their focus off of themselves long enough to see the bigger picture. Death has a unique way of doing that; it sobers us to reality. I once had a brush with death that accomplished this for me. My wife and I were traveling down the I-5 highway in Washington State at 70 MPH when a deer ran in front of our car. I only had time for a high-pitched scream before I plowed into Bambi, sending it heavenward and setting off an airbag explosion in my face. Somehow, I made it safely to the side of the highway, where I examined the deer and investigated the damage to the car. Although my wife and I were fine, the deer was dead and our faithful Toyota Tercel was totaled.

After the accident, I imagined a dozen ways in which it could have ended tragically. The shock of that experience, as with all close calls, did not bring visions of my possessions or a renewed passion for consumerism. In light of death, it became painfully clear what little value stuff has. If you listen to people reflect on death, you will hear a similar story. Recently, I read a blogpost from Death Row Diary, where the sister of a man who was on death row published his sobering thoughts on life:

> When your warrant gets signed so many things suddenly become trivial. I've already thrown or given away 95% of my personal property, the stuff that for years seemed so important. All those great books I'll never get to read; reams and reams of legal work I've been dragging around, and studying, for 2 decades and which has suddenly lost its relevance. My magazines and newspapers stack up unread; I have little appetite

to waste valuable, irreplaceable hours reading up on current events. Does it really matter to me now what's happening in the Middle East, or on Wall Street, or how my Miami Dolphins are looking for the upcoming new season? What's the point? Ditto the TV; I'm uninterested in wasting time watching programs that now mean nothing in the grand scheme of things. The other day I caught myself reaching for my daily vitamin. Really? I wondered, as the absurdity hit me. Likewise, after 40 years of working out religiously, that's out the window now. Again, what's the point?[26]

You'll notice that people who are close to death care the least about the things of this world. Yet, somehow, many of us don't realize that we are all on death row! Last time I checked, human mortality still hovers around 100%. The only thing different with this man is that he knew exactly how and when he was going to die. It's so easy for us to get caught up in living that we forget what's really worth living for. Death has a way of awakening us to the reality of life and bringing what really matters into sharp focus: relationships.

Sadly, most people attempt to fill their restless longing for relationship with God with things that do not satisfy or last. If these other things don't fill us, it stands to reason that God is the only thing that can. This is the conclusion Douglas Coupland arrives at near the end of his book, *Life After God*, saying:

> Now— here is my secret: I tell it to you with an openness of heart that I doubt I shall ever achieve again, so I pray that you are in a quiet room as you hear these words. My secret is that I need God—that I am sick and can no longer make it alone. I need God to help me give,

because I no longer seem to be capable of giving; to help me be kind, as I no longer seem capable of kindness; to help me love, as I seem beyond being able to love.[27]

History is full of men and women who, in the search for meaning, were led to God. Tolstoy was one of them. After describing his dark period of hopelessness, he went on to write:

> ...in the course of a whole year, when almost every minute I was asking myself whether I should end it all with a rope or a bullet, when I was occupied with the thoughts and observations I have described, my heart was tormented with an agonizing feeling. This feeling I can only describe as a search for God... It was a feeling of dread, of loneliness, of forlornness in the midst of all that was alien to me; and it was a feeling of hope for someone's help.[28]

Tolstoy went on to find his help in God. It was a journey that led him to find the meaning he longed for in Jesus Christ. His relationship with God, through Jesus, became a source of inspiration to him, and he wrote some profound works on life and love, which would come to influence both Gandhi and Martin Luther King Jr. They also influenced me. I now seek to find my meaning in relationship with the God who is my hope and help. My relationship with God inspires me to make life investments, not into mutual funds for retirement, but into my relationships for eternity.

In this chapter, you'll notice that I have raised just as many questions as I have attempted to answer. Each of life's big questions are interconnected and build on one another. In this chapter we discussed that two things are necessary in order for life to have meaning: the existence of God and eternal life. By assuming these two things, we were able to appreciate Jesus' answer to the meaning of life. But are those assumptions true and does Jesus' answer make sense of life's toughest questions? Not surprisingly, any attempt to understand the meaning of life naturally leads to a search for the author—a search for God. So, in the next chapter we will ask the question: "Does God Exist?"

THINKING?

Chapter Two

Does God Exist?

A 1987 Jeep Wrangler and a couple of boxes in the back seat made up all of my earthly belongings the day I left home to go to college. Packing up my childhood possessions marked an important transition into adulthood; I spent most of the day deliberating over which memorabilia would be stored in the garage and which would come with me. Not much made the cut! At the end of the day, my mom and stepdad came out onto the driveway to wish me off. It was one of those moments I will never forget. With tears in her eyes, my mom gave me a big hug and a kiss and wished me well on my journey. It was difficult to leave, but exciting at the same time. I shut my car door, gave a quick wave, and was off to face the world.

In time, I began to appreciate that it was much more than just my belongings I was picking through that day as I left for college—it was also my beliefs. Leaving home begins a process in which we deliberate over the beliefs we have collected in our youth and begin to determine which ones will get packed up and left behind and which will come along with us. It's a journey that we all embark on as we develop our worldview.

A worldview is like a pair of glasses that affects how each person uniquely views the world. It encompasses all of our assumptions and beliefs, from the most mundane to the most profound, from our feelings about chocolate milkshakes to our understanding of gravity, politics, or education. Whether we are aware of it or not, we all have a distinct view of the world pieced together from our experiences and the facts we gather along the way. What we need to ask then, is not whether we have a worldview, but rather how closely our current worldview resembles reality. Do we have sound evidence for our beliefs about life? Or, as the ancient Greek thinker Plato (423-348 BC) put it: is what you believe true, good, and beautiful?[1]

When I arrived at college, it didn't take long for me to realize that not all my beliefs about the world were true or good—and they were definitely not all beautiful! This became clear to me four months into college life, when a purplish substance suddenly appeared in my toilet. I confronted my three roommates with whom I shared a bathroom. I thought that maybe someone had spilt paint in the toilet bowl and not bothered to clean it up. Through their laughter, my roommates explained to me, with a sense of pride, that together we had been growing mold! I was appalled. I had no idea that a toilet had an expiration date, after which it must be cleaned; I guess my worldview just assumed that toilets were self-cleaning. It was equally disturbing to discover that there are people in this world that would enjoy growing mold in their toilet. I promptly cleaned it.

Not long after that, I learned that bed sheets, like clothes, need to be washed regularly! This was news to me as well. As you can imagine, I had not previously appreciated all that my mom had done for me growing up, but now my worldview was expanding, and I think you would agree that it was for the better. In college, I began to re-think all of my beliefs, from the small to the large, and because of this I was beginning to see the world differently.

The goal of any worldview is to see the world correctly. In fact, this is often how truth is defined; truth is that which correctly corresponds to reality. Plato's student, Aristotle (384-322 BC), once wrote that, "all men by nature desire to know."[2] I think he's right; but what is it that we desire to know? Do we want to know the truth?

I want to see the world correctly—the way it really is.

My Mom and God

One of the views of the world that I had inherited growing up concerned God. Shortly before my parents separated, my mom had become a Christian. Her relationship with God not only brought her life meaning, but it also became her source of beauty and strength; it had a way of infusing her with passion for life and a love for other people. As I was growing up, I watched my mom's relationship with God and that helped form my own Christian worldview.

However, when I moved away from home and went to college, I was confronted with the reality of my beliefs. No one was dragging me to church. I no longer needed to pray before meals. These were now my choices. How would I live? Everyone is eventually faced with this problem, when you realize that what you believe about the world has a direct impact on the way you live in it. So, one day I confronted myself on the inconsistencies of my beliefs and actions. "Andy," I said, "Do you really believe that God exists? I mean *really* believe it?" It was a life-changing question.

In the last chapter, we discovered that God's existence is necessary for life to have objective meaning. If Jesus is correct that the meaning of life is about relationship with God and how that relationship with God inspires us to love others, it will change the way you see and live in the world. For this reason, I wanted to know if God truly existed, because if he did, I wanted to know this God like my mom did. I wanted a relationship with God—but not an imaginary relationship. I wanted to experience reality correctly—the truth about God.

Prove It

Statistics consistently demonstrate that the vast majority of the world's population believes that a God does exist.[3] It's a belief that doesn't need to be taught and seems to come naturally to humankind. Research even indicates that this is true of children; we're born with a bent toward *believing* in a God or gods.[4] But, of course, that doesn't mean it's true. After all, I initially believed that toilets cleaned themselves and that certainly wasn't true! Likewise, while I was attracted to God because of how I saw him reflected in my mother's life, that alone didn't prove the existence of God. It merely provided evidence for the therapeutic effect of *believing in* a God. I also see God poorly reflected in people's lives, but again what does that prove? It might help prove the fickleness of people, but certainly not the non-existence of God. How then can we determine if God does or does not exist? Can his existence be proven with absolute 100% certainty?

The problem is that there are few things, if any, that we can prove with that level of confidence. Perhaps it's because the implications of God's existence are so profound, but we tend to demand a greater level of certainty for God's existence than we would for anything else.

The rules of logic remind us that 100% proof doesn't exist for any of our most basic and cherished beliefs. For example, think of the movie *The Matrix*, starring Keanu Reeves. In the movie, the "reality" all humans perceive with their five senses is really just an elaborate computer simulation called the Matrix, which was set up and maintained by sentient machines that had rebelled against humankind. The humans living in the Matrix are unaware that they are in a simulation, and it's only by taking a red pill that they "wake up" and realize the truth about the world.

With that in mind, the question is: can you prove 100% that your body exists in the real world and that you're not just living in a computer simulation like the Matrix?

Really. Take some time and think about it.

As frightening as it is, that question is not a new one. While *The Matrix* popularized it, the concept of humans being unaware of true reality has been intriguing philosophers for centuries. Plato wondered if perhaps human reality is like being stuck in a cave and watching shadows dance on the wall, with the true reality happening just outside of our perception.[5] The French philosopher René Descartes (1596-1650) suggested that there could be an evil demon who has deluded all of our senses, making us think that we have a body and that there is an external world, when in reality, there is neither.[6] More recently, Swedish philosopher Nick Bostrom at Oxford has come up with the "simulation argument," in which he attempts to mathematically predict the likelihood that our reality is actually a computer simulation set up by more advanced civilizations.[7]

Why do all of these people keep waxing on about something that seems obviously false to the rest of us? Of course, we don't live in a computer simulation! The problem is that we can't really prove it. Not 100%. To that level of certainty, we can't prove that we exist, that our senses are trustworthy, that our capacity for reason is dependable, or any of our other most basic beliefs. Perhaps the most certain I can be about anything is summarized in Descartes' famous axiom, "I think, therefore I am."[8] Basically, it means that if there is one thing that I can surely be confident of, it is that I am thinking, and if I am thinking, then I must exist. After all, the very act of doubting your own existence would merely prove that you have a mind, and therefore, that you do exist. Beyond that, proving anything in this world 100% is nearly impossible.

So, if it is the case that proving anything is so difficult, why do we demand that level of certainty for the existence of God? This is especially troubling when you realize that not only can you not prove God's existence, but also you can't *disprove* God's existence either. Instead we need to adjust our definition of "proof." It's far more realistic to look for evidence that demonstrates God's existence is *reasonable*. After all, this is how we determine all of our beliefs. Even though I can't prove that I don't live in the Matrix, I have good reasons to believe that I don't.

Notice that this is how our justice system works. In a criminal investigation, there is never an *absolute* certainty of 'who dunnit,' only degrees of likelihood upon which a case is built and a jury deliberates. After all, even if a suspect confesses to the crime, there is always the possibility, however remote, that they are lying. Therefore, the standard of the jury's judgment in a criminal conviction is: beyond all *reasonable* doubt. This is how all of our beliefs are developed, including the belief that God exists.

It's easy to misunderstand this point, so I'll clarify what I'm not saying. I'm not saying that you can't be absolutely confident in your belief in God. I believe you can. I just don't believe that you can *prove* that belief with absolute certainty, nor do I believe you need to.

When we ask "Does God exist?," we are seeking to examine the evidence and determine in which direction the scales are tipping, be it ever so slightly or significantly in favor of God's existence or not. Tipping our personal scales becomes a verdict for belief. Like a scale, the more evidence we accumulate, the weightier our convictions grow. This is why, according to the Christian worldview, faith can be defined as: trusting what you have good reason to believe is true.

So, what amounts to good reason?

Or, in other words, how much certainty do *you* need before *you* believe? That's a personal question. It's why we can have a hung jury. People look at the same evidence, but have different standards as to when the verdict becomes "reasonable."

Does Sasquatch Exist?

In philosophy, the study of truth or knowledge is called epistemology. Epistemology teaches us that the evidence we gather will mainly come in two forms: facts and experience. Christianity is unique in that it offers both forms of knowledge to demonstrate the reasonableness of God's existence. We can study the factual evidence for God's existence; it's testable. Also, we can actually experience the person of God; he's relational. There are, however, some things to watch out for.

Consider Sasquatch for a moment. It may sadden some readers to know that I have come to the belief that Sasquatch does not exist. Now, I have not come to this conclusion lightly. I, like many before me, have watched numerous TV shows about Big Foot and Yeti. While hiking in the Pacific Northwest, I have always kept a watchful eye out for this hairy ape and in the Himalayas of Nepal, I even paid $3 for some Buddhist monks to show me what they claimed was the skull of a Yeti. Yet, after all the evidence was weighed, I was just not convinced.

How did I arrive at this conclusion? My belief was not formed by a single piece of evidence, but rather by the accumulation of multiple lines of evidence. This is referred to as a *cumulative* case: many pieces of evidence working together to form a single reasonable conclusion. It's important to understand that the idea of blind faith is a foreign concept in the Christian tradition. Christianity has always been a knowledge tradition in which the case for God has been, and continues to be, developed from facts and experience. Thousands of years ago, the psalmist David wrote that the universe screams at us the truth of God's existence:

The heavens declare the glory of God;
the skies proclaim the work of his hands.
Day after day they pour forth speech;
night after night they reveal knowledge.
They have no speech, they use no words;
no sound is heard from them.
Yet, their voice goes out into all the earth,
their words to the ends of the world.[9]

Thus, Christians believe that the universe, which God made, is full of evidence that points towards him. This is what a cumulative case seeks to accomplish: to find all of the evidence and see if it is plainly or clearly pointing to the same conclusion.

Now this is where things get weird and we need to take care. People tend not to treat all evidence equally. Imagine with me for a moment that a good friend of mine, with whom I have been on countless hiking trips and who I trust deeply, were to tell me a dramatic account of a recent experience he had in the wilderness—with Sasquatch. Imagine that he was utterly sincere, not just trying to pull my leg. I think you would agree that his five-minute story would do more to challenge my belief than an hour-long documentary on TV or some monks showing me a coconut with fur glued on it ever could.[10] Or consider when a spouse has been cheated on. A husband or a wife could be confronted with plenty of factual evidence for their spouse's infidelity, but refuse to believe it because of their experience. They may not want to believe it, or their experience may be one of such love and devotion that they just cannot believe it. But then, one day they come home early from work and see the truth for themselves and their experience changes their belief. Experience, both positive and negative, can powerfully persuade us. Why is that?

Simply put, people are more convinced by their own experiences, and the experiences of others they trust, than they are by factual evidence alone. I think this is because we are relational creatures, but whatever the reason, we need to be careful. Experience isn't an invalid form of knowledge, but it is important to remember that facts and experience need to work together in order to develop a well-grounded belief. Your experiences, or the experience of others you trust, could be wrong.

Observing the experience of others had some interesting consequences in my own search for God. When I went off to college, I developed many trusted relationships with agnostics, atheists, and people of other faiths. All of these friends had experiences that defined their beliefs; yet, their beliefs couldn't all be true, since they wildly contradicted each other. Although it was difficult, I realized it was important to look beyond my own personal experience, or the personal experience of anyone else, to see the objective facts which could provide evidence for or against God.

Bias?

I have found that discussing the existence of God with those who hold competing beliefs can be incredibly complicated and potentially confusing. Often, we think we are having a conversation about God, when in fact we are just talking past each other. This is because people approach the question of God's existence in different ways. One common approach is arriving at a conclusion even before the question is posed. It was a long, frustrating conversation with an atheistic friend of mine that helped me to appreciate this point. He had dismissed every piece of factual and experiential evidence I had shared to support why I believe in God. I finally gave up trying to persuade him and asked, "Ben, could you even be convinced that God exists?" Without hesitation, Ben replied, "Yes, I think so." "Okay," I said, "what would it take to convince you?" Ben leaned back in his chair, folded his hands behind his head, and looked up at the ceiling in contemplation. After some reflection, Ben replied, "I don't know." I wasn't surprised. "Ben," I said, "I don't think anything can convince you." Ben looked shocked as I went on, "What if God ripped the roof off this building right now and appeared in front of you saying, 'Guess who?' Besides being totally freaked out, you would probably just assume that someone spiked your brownies, that you were dreaming, or that you had lost your mind. The fact is, I'm not sure I can even think of a way that God could reveal himself to you that you couldn't reason your way out of." To this, Ben responded, "Yeah, I guess you're right."

You see, my friend Ben had assumed that God didn't exist even before we had started looking at the evidence. He had answered the question even before it had been asked. When he was honest with himself, he recognized it. This is why the issue of worldviews is so important. Before we can talk about the existence of God, we first need to ask ourselves if God is even an option within our current worldview. In many people's worldview, he isn't.

From my experience, people approach the question of God's existence from one of two positions: an open or a closed universe. An open universe is one in which people admit that something could exist beyond the physical universe, perhaps even interact within it. On the contrary, a closed universe is the belief that the physical universe is all that exists and can be known. This belief is often called physicalism[11] and is summed up neatly by Carl Sagan who said, "the cosmos is all that is, or ever was, or ever will be."[12]

At its very core, physicalism requires a level of knowledge that is impossible to attain. How could you ever know that the physical world is all there is (that it's closed)? If we can't prove that the universe is all there is, shouldn't we at least remain open to the possibility of something else? I think that, based on the evidence, the only reasonable position to hold is that the universe could be open. A person that holds this view can potentially be convinced that God exists and that life has an author.

I Believe in Science

Notice that if your worldview is committed to physicalism, then, like my friend Ben, no amount of evidence for God will ever be enough. It's not even a possible answer and therefore, can never receive a fair hearing. Often, I hear people of the physicalist persuasion triumphantly declare, "I believe in science!" as though science is some sort of higher ground or brute fact that contains access to all of life's answers while avoiding the weaknesses of faith.

If only life were that simple!

Faith plays a fundamental role in everything, including science. Specifically, science rests on a foundation of faith, namely the belief that the universe we observe is rationally intelligible. If you want to use science to test the world in order to gain knowledge, you must first assume that the world you are observing and testing is being understood correctly by your senses. But how do you prove that? You can't—in just the same way as you can't prove that you don't live in the Matrix. Instead, you take it on faith. This raises the question: what good reason do you have that your senses are working correctly?

You see, it's long been trumpeted that people coming from a religious background have a bias toward wanting to believe in God, and it is expected that they will skew the evidence so that it lines up with that bias. It is presumed that non-religious people don't have those same biases and can look at the facts more objectively. However, understanding physicalism reveals that it is just as strong a bias. It isn't the result of consulting the evidence, rather it assumes the answer it wants about God before it even asks the question. Many scientists who adamantly reject the notion of God have admitted this.[13]

The truth is, we all have biases, assumptions based on our worldviews, which will tempt us to find only what we want to find. Yet, by acknowledging these biases, we can determine to follow the evidence wherever it leads, either towards or away from a belief in God's existence. Strict adherence to physicalism doesn't allow this.

Rethink History

If we believe that the universe could be open, and if we are willing to acknowledge our biases and try to move past them, then we can really start to examine the evidence for or against God. But before we take a look at evidence for God, we first need to do some myth-busting.

It's important to note that science actually got its start and motivation from religious beliefs. The Judeo-Christian worldview had always taught that one God exists and that he created everything. It was believed that God had revealed himself in two primary ways: the work that he had done in nature and the words that he had spoken in scripture.[14] It stood to follow that if we were required to study the Bible, then surely we were required to study nature as well. In a similar way, Christianity had always taught that God is good, he is not trying to trick us, and that he is orderly, having created uniform laws that nature must follow. This understanding of God was key to concluding that we have good reason to trust our five senses and a warrant to seek out these natural laws. It followed that if we could trust our senses, then we could test the world around us and expect to find truth. It was in this theologically fertile soil of the sixteenth and seventeenth centuries that modern science took root and the Scientific Revolution began, ultimately kick-starting the Enlightenment.[15]

Yet, today many people believe that science and religion are enemies.

This is just plain false.

Christianity is not anti-science. Rather, the Judeo-Christian worldview is the one that conceived of modern science in the first place and has always had a robust scientific tradition. In fact, for the fathers of science—Copernicus, Galileo, Kepler, and Newton—their belief in God is what motivated them to study the universe. Johannes Kepler (1571-1630) was an influential German astronomer and mathematician best known for articulating the laws of planetary motion. His love for God not only personally compelled him to study the world, but he also claimed that all people should embrace science because it is a gift from God and reveals something of God's character. He said:

> It is a right, yes a duty, to search in cautious manner for the numbers, sizes, and weights, the norms for everything [God] has created. For He himself has let man take part in the knowledge of these things... For these secrets are not of the kind whose research should

be forbidden; rather they are set before our eyes like a mirror so that by examining them we observe to some extent the goodness and wisdom of the Creator.[16]

Far from divorcing God and science, Kepler's study of the planets was a way for him to marvel and worship the One who created them.[17] As he famously put it, science was an attempt to "think God's thoughts after him."

The reality is that not everything you have been taught about history is true. For example, besides maybe a few oddballs, no one in antiquity actually believed that the earth was flat. Not even Columbus believed that! Sure, he thought the earth was much smaller than it is, but lots of people disagreed with him. The fact is, the Greeks knew the earth was round, and were able to calculate its circumference pretty accurately about 500 years before Christ's birth! Yet, we are often led to believe in the bravery of Columbus, who sailed west despite believing he might sail off the edge of the world. In truth, that's just nonsense.[18]

Likewise, the belief that science and religion are fundamentally opposed to each other is a commonly held belief that is just plain false. Prior to the late 1800s, nobody, either theist or atheist, believed that science and religion were intrinsically at odds. Then two men, John William Draper and Andrew Dickson White, together invented the "conflict thesis," which suggested that science and Christianity had been continually fighting one another through the centuries.[19] This idea was immediately criticized by scholars, who accused it of being founded on myth and fabrication.[20] Yet, somehow it caught the attention of the public, and it began to be widely taught. Among scholars, support for the conflict thesis continued to decline steadily, until it reached the point where, currently, *no historian considers it valid*. Yet, despite being debunked many years ago, most people still believe this myth that science and religion are at war.[21]

Far from science not needing God, it is God that gives science its rational starting point. Science and faith aren't fighting; they are working together. John Polkinghorne, an Anglican priest and theoretical physicist from Cambridge, explains this relationship beautifully:

> Why, then, do I believe in these invisible quarks?...In summary, it's because quarks make sense of a lot of direct physical experience...I wish to engage in a similar strategy with regard to the unseen reality of God. God's existence makes sense of many aspects of our knowledge and experience...I do not believe that I shift gear in some strange intellectual way when I move from science to religion...In their search for truth, science and religion are intellectual cousins under the skin.[22]

So, the problem is not that something within science and religion makes them innately irreconcilable. If that were the case, we would expect that all successful scientists would be atheists. They would have to be in order to do good science. However, in the top echelons of science, we find that this simply isn't the case. Analysis of Nobel Prize winners shows that, between the years 1901 and 2000, Christians won 74.0% of the prizes in chemistry, 65.3% in physics, and 64.3% in medicine.[23] In contrast, Atheists, Agnostics, and Freethinkers won just 7.1%, 4.8%, and 8.9% in the same categories, respectively. Those statistics certainly don't give much credence to the conflict theory.

The problem is that some people, for various reasons, want to divorce science and religion and create a world completely dependent on science. What they may or may not realize is that in doing so, they have committed themselves, by faith, to a purely physical view of the world—a view that has some bizarre consequences. This new religion of sorts is often called scientism, and it's a worldview that contains some significant challenges.

Pressure Cooker Bomb

In order to appreciate the worldview limitations of scientism, let's consider how science helps at a crime scene. On April 15th, 2013, at 2:49PM, two explosions rocked the Boston Marathon, killing three people and injuring over 250 others. Whenever tragedy strikes, there are some basic questions that all people want answered. The first question is *how*—how did this happen?

Science is an amazing tool for answering *how* questions. When that explosion ripped through those marathon runners that day, the police quickly cordoned off a twelve-block radius and set to work on answering that question. It didn't take long to discover the remains of two pressure cooker bombs. This wasn't the site of a natural disaster or a freak accident. It was a crime scene!

Now, could you imagine if the investigation had ended there? The police could have held a media briefing to reconstruct the blast, giving detailed descriptions of the physics behind the bombs detonating and the shock waves of shrapnel that flew through the crowd. But would people have been satisfied? No way! People wanted answers and "how did this happen?" was only the beginning. The second question was *who*—who was responsible?

The FBI set to work collecting evidence and three days later, on April 18th, they announced that they believed two brothers to be responsible for the explosives. The brothers were quickly located and a shootout ensued, leaving one of the suspects dead and the other injured and on the run. In order to find him, one of the greatest manhunts in U.S. history was organized in Watertown, Massachusetts; everyone was ordered to stay inside while thousands of officers combed the streets. On April 19th, the injured brother was found hiding in a resident's backyard and was taken into custody.

Again, consider if the police had stopped there. We knew how it had happened and who did it. Was that enough? Of course not! We wanted justice, but we also wanted more than that. Could you imagine watching a crime show on TV that ended once the suspects were caught and convicted? No one would watch it! Instead, this type of show is interested in the same thing we are: answering the *why* question—why did they do it?

It turns out that the brothers were self-radicalized Islamic extremists who were planning to bomb Times Square next. Have you ever noticed that the *why* question is the one we find the most important and interesting? Everything comes down to motive. Yet, this is where the problem with scientism surfaces. On the day of the Boston Marathon bombings, no amount of scientific inquiry could explain why two brothers would do that. Just as no amount of study could decipher the meaning of Egyptian Hieroglyphics, science alone cannot answer the *why* questions.

THINKING?

The Limits of Science

The Enlightenment demonstrated the helpfulness of science, but it also taught us its limitations. During the 1600s, knowledge of the world exploded as interest in science increased, but eventually, people began to ask too much of science. Putting all their hope into this budding discipline, people naïvely believed that it would answer all of life's questions. This is a belief that many still hold today, such as chemist Peter Atkins, who said, "There is no reason to suppose that science cannot deal with every aspect of existence."[24]

Yet, as in the case of the Boston Marathon Bombing, science just isn't equipped to answer every question, especially the *who* and *why* questions. Biologist Sir Peter Medawar says:

> There is no quicker way for a scientist to bring discredit upon himself and on his profession than roundly to declare that science knows or soon will know the answers to all questions worth asking...[it] falls short of answering the many simple and childlike questions people like to ask: questions about origins and purposes.[25]

This point was made frustratingly clear to me during a trip to the Vatican. My wife and I were celebrating our tenth wedding anniversary with a trip to Italy. Rome is well-known for its priceless artifacts and artwork, but the one thing I was most looking forward to seeing was Raphael's masterpiece, *The School of Athens*.

Like cattle, we were herded through the Vatican, from room to room, until we finally reached the home of the famous fresco. Eagerly I began to study it, only to realize that I had no idea what I was looking at! What did it all mean? Sure, I'm not an art historian, but *The School of Athens* is so packed with meaning that it confuses even experts. Thankfully, my wife had talked me into renting an audio guide, which could give us information about the painting. I placed the little device to my ear and a digital voice told me lots of important details; I learned when it was painted, how it was painted, and how long it took. Yet, even after learning all of these details, I was still disappointed; it felt insufficient. Knowing *about* something is not the same as knowing *why* something.

What I really wanted was Raphael himself standing beside me explaining the meaning and purpose behind each brush-stroke: who were the characters, what did they represent, and what significance was there in their placement? For example, we know that after the painting was complete, Raphael went back and painted Michelangelo, his biggest rival, into the forefront, in such a way as to make him sit geometrically out-of-sync with all of the other figures. Why would he do this? Scholars can guess at these answers, but as we saw in chapter one, if we want to know true objective meaning, we have to ask the author.

The truth is: science has limitations. Science can explain how the painting was made and even analyze the fresco down to its atoms, but never arrive at why it was made. More than that, science can never determine if the fresco is a priceless work of art or complete garbage, a beautiful masterpiece or an ugly wall.

The same is true of the Boston Bombing. Science can tell you how a pressure cooker bomb works, but not whether you should detonate one at a marathon.

Simply explaining how the universe works will never satisfy us.

Rather than having science be the answer to our questions, a role it is incapable of filling, let's instead use science as a helpful tool in our search for answers. Just as science provided the police with evidence after the explosion in Boston, science can help us examine the evidence after another explosion—the Big Bang. In Boston, the evidence pointed to a person as the cause. Perhaps the same is true of the universe? Let's turn now to the telescope and the microscope and examine some evidence for God.

Evidence from the Telescope

I remember clearly the first time I looked through a telescope. When I was in middle school, I had a good friend whose father was an amateur astronomer. They lived far enough away from the city to be free from light pollution and, one evening, they set the telescope up on the front lawn. I climbed up on a little stool, peered into the lens, and there it was: Saturn! 1.2 billion kilometers away and we could see it clear as day—even the rings. It was awe-inspiring. A few minutes later, he swung the telescope around and aimed it at the Milky Way, a hazy streak of light in the sky—it was all stars! I had no idea that the Milky Way was made up of billions of stars!

Besides the sun, the closest star to earth is Proxima Centauri. If we travelled at the speed of light, it would take over four years to get there. Four light years! That's unbelievably far; yet, to travel completely across our Milky Way Galaxy would take over 100,000 light years.[26] That's unfathomable to me! Yet, if that's how big our galaxy is, what about the size of the entire universe?

Modern astronomy has revealed a complex and immense universe that defies human comprehension. Have you ever wondered just how big the universe is? Well, some astronomers decided to do an experiment to find out.[27] They pointed the Hubble Space

Telescope into a small square section of black space and started taking pictures. They returned regularly over the next ten years, until they had over 2,000 images. What did they find? In that small square of black space, they counted over 5,500 new galaxies that had never been seen before, each of which contains billions of stars! In total, scientists now estimate that the observable universe contains 100-200 billion galaxies—and that's just the observable universe! They are convinced there is more out there that we just can't see. Meanwhile, here we sit: in a small galaxy, on a tiny blue rock, orbiting a massive burning star. Disturbed? I am! Shouldn't we all be amazed that we find ourselves in such a predicament? I mean, have you ever considered where all this came from and how we got here?

A Roman Catholic priest and scientist named Georges Lemaître (1894-1966) thought long and hard about this question. In 1927, he became the first to propose the theory of an expanding universe, a theory that would later be adopted universally among scientists and coined the Big Bang. Essentially, the Big Bang theory revealed that the universe began as an infinitely dense singularity, a starting point, which exploded, has been expanding ever since, and will continue to expand until all of its energy is expelled. This was a huge discovery that made the questions of our origin even more amazing! Until this point, scientists had believed that the universe was eternal, an idea we inherited from Aristotle. Now, science had revealed that the universe had a beginning and an end. Naturally, the question arose, what or who is responsible?

The Kalam Cosmological Argument, popularized by William Lane Craig, puts the problem of the origin of the universe like this:

1) Whatever begins to exist has a cause.
2) The universe began to exist.
3) Therefore, the universe has a cause.

Just like a crime scene, whenever there's an explosion, we study the evidence to deduce what the cause was. Remember what we talked about earlier: some people believe the physical universe is all that exists (closed universe), while others believe that there could be something that exists beyond the physical (open universe). Now think for a moment. If the physical universe is all that exists, then what was there before the physical universe came into existence?

There was nothing!

Well then, what caused the universe to come into existence?

Nothing?

Some people suggest that the universe caused itself, that it came from nothing, by nothing, and for nothing.[28] Logic, however, tells us that from nothing you get...nothing! To think that nothing caused something is just absurd.

Christianity refers to the explosion of the universe into existence as creation *ex nihilo*—'from nothing.' However, Christianity doesn't mean that the universe came from nothing, but rather that it came from nothing *physical*. In that case, what created the universe? Genesis 1:1 tells us that, "In the beginning God created the heavens and the earth." This worldview proposes that before the universe came into being, there was nothing physical. Instead there was something non-physical and eternal—God.

Often, I hear people object to this conclusion, asking, "Okay then, who created God?" It's important not to draw a false comparison. Notice that the universe must have had a cause because it had a beginning; it *came into* existence. God, on the other hand, does not have a birthdate, he did not come into existence, and so no cause is required. As the first premise of the Kalam Cosmological Argument says, only what *begins to exist* needs a cause.

Now some people will claim that God being eternal is absurd or special pleading.[29] Is it even possible for something to be eternal? Yet, consider that up until a hundred years ago, the dominant worldview held that the universe was eternal. Nobody seemed to have a problem with that view until the evidence demonstrated otherwise!

More and more, I hear people pointing toward quantum mechanics as a possible explanation for how you can get something from nothing. Granted, we do see some incredible things at the quantum level, but what we have never seen is creation ex nihilo (from nothing). William Lane Craig explains the problem with this view well:

> The quantum vacuum is not what most people envision when they think of a vacuum—that is, absolutely nothing. On the contrary, it's a sea of fluctuating energy, an arena of violent activity that has a rich physical structure and can be described by physical laws...We have to ask, well, what is the origin of the whole quantum vacuum itself? Where does it come from?...You've simply pushed back the issue of creation. Now you've got to account for how this very active ocean of fluctuating energy came into being.[30]

It is true that quantum fluctuations can occur with seemingly no cause whatsoever. However, that's not the point of this argument. The premise is that whatever *begins to exist* has a cause: quantum mechanics came into existence during the Big Bang, therefore it can't be the cause. Something can't bring itself into existence. This is the problem with all of science's supposed solutions to the creation problem, from the oscillating model to the multiverse. Like it or not, eventually there needs to be an eternal, uncaused cause, something that has the attributes of God. Otherwise, you end up with an infinite regress of causes—you begin the absurd, never-ending inquiry of asking, "what caused *that*? OK, what caused *that*?" You get the point. Therefore, there is good reason to conclude that God is the foundation from which everything else came.

Who is this First Cause?

Like a crime scene, the more I peer through the telescope, the more I find myself asking, "who did it?" William Lane Craig concludes from the evidence cited above that there is a "necessary, uncaused, timeless, spaceless, immaterial personal Creator of the universe."[31] The first time I heard this, I was surprised. It seemed clear that the evidence was pointing to a creator, but how do we know that the creator is personal or relational and not an impersonal force?

I learned that when it comes to non-physical causes, there are only two options: the cause is either impersonal (such as an abstract object like the laws of mathematics), or it's personal (such as an unembodied mind). The problem is that abstract objects, like laws, can't cause things. As mathematician John Lennox humorously put it, "in the world in which most of us live, the simple law of arithmetic 1+1=2, never brought anything into being by itself. It certainly has never put any money into my bank account."[32] Therefore, the cause must be personal. The only thing we know of that is both non-physical and capable of causing anything as a first cause is a person; only personal beings are capable of having wills which can act on the universe.

Further, this is what Christianity has always said about God; the Bible asserts that the natural world reveals not only the existence of God, but his personal character as well. Romans 1:19-20 says:

> Since what may be known about God is plain to them, because God has made it plain to them. For since the creation of the world God's invisible qualities—his eternal power and divine nature—have been clearly seen, being understood from what has been made...

The Apostle Paul, who wrote those words, confirmed that the God who made the universe is the same personal God who loves us.

The universe we live in is truly amazing. You might even refer to it as a miracle. Yet, there is a miracle even greater than existence and that's to *know* that you exist. Albert Einstein put it like this, "The most incomprehensible thing about the universe is that it is comprehensible."[33] It's amazing to think that we are not only aware of our existence, but that we can also study the world and understand it. It's not beyond us. Peering into the night sky with a telescope has brought me to something personal and relational in nature—a God that I can comprehend.

Evidence from the Microscope

Now, I want to turn our attention from the grand to the minuscule by looking into the microscope to see what our existence can tell us about God.

The first time I peered through a microscope was in my high school biology class and it opened my mind to a whole other world. The universe isn't only immeasurably big—it's also extremely small! In fact, it's difficult to believe, but the world is nearly as small as it is large. Whether you look out or in, the universe will astonish you.

The intricacies of life at the smallest level have always amazed me. This fascination with biology only grew stronger one day in biology class, when I was greeted by the unpleasant odor of formaldehyde. As I took my seat, I was welcomed by a dead frog awaiting my scalpel. The art of dissection reminded me of being a kid; when I was younger, I had the habit of taking things apart all around our house, only to realize that I could never put them back together again. My poor mother nearly went mad from my destructive curiosity. As I took apart that frog, I was both disturbed and awestruck. Clearly, this was much more complex than taking apart a toaster!

Over the last century, the curiosity of scientific discovery has led biologists to 'disassemble' human life down to the molecular level. In the process, they discovered a world of unfathomable complexity. For a long time, we have known about our organs and tissues, but the advancement of the microscope has revealed the further details of cells, proteins, and amino acids.

The basic components for all living things, from the gigantic to the minuscule, are amino acids; they are the "nuts and bolts" that when arranged or sequenced correctly, make up proteins. Proteins in turn, make up the parts of a living cell. Cells are what comprise tissue; tissues form organs; and organs function together to form an organism, such as a human.

There are around twenty different amino acids that are found in life.[34] In order to form a protein, 150–3,000 amino acids must be ordered into the correct sequence. Then, between 250–3,000 proteins must be organized in order to form a living cell—the very simplest form of life on earth. As you can begin to appreciate, humans are incredibly complex and information-rich, even at our most basic level.

The question that jumps to my mind is this: how on earth do all of those amino acids get sequenced correctly to create proteins?

The answer is DNA.

DNA (deoxyribonucleic acid) are long strings that contain all the information needed to make proteins, like a blueprint showing how to construct a person. The Human Genome Project, led by Christian scientist Francis Collins, was the world's largest biological project. It was responsible for mapping the human genome contained within DNA. The scope of this project was immense! It might surprise you to learn that human DNA is a code that is over three billion letters long—and that's just one strand of DNA! Consider that the diameter of a DNA molecule is only two nanometers, while the average diameter of a human hair is around 100,000 nanometers. It has been calculated that a single teaspoon could hold one strand of DNA from every species that has ever existed and still have room for the information from every book that has ever been written![35] Speaking of books, if your DNA were an instruction manual, it would be approximately 1,000,000 pages long, single-spaced in 12-point font.

Obviously, referring to DNA as complex is an understatement.

Current scientific discoveries have only revealed a fraction of the information found in that code. As Bill Gates said, "DNA is like a computer program, but far, far more advanced than any software we've ever created."[36]

So, the obvious question is: where did the information found in DNA come from? Scientism, which cannot accept non-naturalistic answers, insists that a natural, unguided process, such as non-theistic evolution, is completely responsible for the origin of life.[37] Yet, the problem with that answer is that the very function of evolution is dependent on the existence of an organism with self-replicating DNA; without genetic material, which has the ability to mutate, natural selection grinds to a halt. Therefore, naturalistic evolution simply cannot account for the origin of the genetic material in the first place.[38]

Skeptics admit that the immense complexity of nature, like DNA, make it appear designed, but they continue to assert that that appearance is false. But why is that? As discussed, *how* questions should be allowed to lead us to *who* and *why* questions. It seems like the simplest and most intuitive answer is that DNA looks designed because it is designed. The evidence from the microscope points toward an author of life.

What Am I?

The biological complexity of DNA is a part of the incredible cumulative evidence pointing to the existence of God, but it also points to much more than that. The truly astounding part of DNA is that despite all of modern research, nowhere have we found the secret to the greatest mystery of all—what makes you, YOU. The more we study DNA, the greater the conviction that we are more than our DNA. It's self-evident to me that although I'm coded for life, my life is not fully coded. I am a person, with a unique mind and the freedom to make choices. You could map my genome perfectly, and yet still not be able to peer into my worldview. You could read my biological instruction manual, and still not know me. DNA may reveal my physical qualities, but it can't reveal the non-physical entities that we call the mind or the soul, that which makes us who we are: a beautifully complex creature, immensely valuable and desiring relationship—a person.

It's incredible to think that you don't need to explain to a child that they are a person; it is something that they are directly aware of. How is that possible? Have you ever considered that although all the cells in our body are replaced approximately every seven years, we remain the same person? How is it that a collection of amino acids is capable of having thoughts about amino acids? How is it possible that you could know my physiology perfectly yet never gain access to what it's like to be me? All of these questions raise the ultimate biological question: what is a person?

Zombie Culture

These days, it seems that zombies are all the rage. They have invaded our novels, our movies, and our TV shows. They have even become a part of everyday life. People now participate in zombie walks, zombie protesting, and zombie proms. However, this recent interest in zombies is not a new phenomenon; zombies have been a part of the human story from the beginning and can be found in different cultures around the world.

I think the interest in zombies stems from a natural fascination with ourselves and what makes us human. Zombies have provided much for us in the way of thought experiments, as we attempt to define what we are by describing what we are not. After all, what is the difference between a zombie and a human? A zombie is commonly thought of as a body that lacks a mind or a soul—it is the dead walking. The idea of zombies, therefore, demands recognition that to be a true person you must have a level of consciousness which is separate from your body. Marcel Proust (1871-1922), a French novelist, put it like this:

> It is in moments of illness that we are compelled to recognize that we live not alone but chained to a creature of a different kingdom, whole worlds apart, who has no knowledge of us and by whom it is impossible to make ourselves understood: our body.[39]

Basically, Proust recognizes that we are not merely bodies. Our true self is totally different and at times, even feels alien to our bodies.

Unfortunately, the issue of consciousness is a difficult thing to study; because we are immersed in it, we have no external vantage point from which to observe. It would be like asking a goldfish what it's like to be wet. Because the goldfish only knows wetness, it is unable to describe or understand it. In a similar way, people have difficulty understanding personhood or consciousness because it's what we're immersed in; we may experience it constantly, and yet it's still a complete mystery. David Charmers, a well-known philosopher of mind from Australia says, "Consciousness poses the most baffling of problems in the science of mind. There is nothing that we know more intimately than conscious experience, but there is nothing that is harder to explain."[40]

Fascinatingly, scientists have not agreed upon a definition of consciousness. Yet, even the least educated among us is a master at detecting it. After all, we don't have any trouble knowing whether a rock is conscious or not, nor do we struggle to know when a person has lost consciousness.

It is not surprising then that we are fascinated by the idea of how a human body would act without consciousness, without personhood. Zombies fill our imaginations with horror and terror, because through them, we seek a vantage point from which to understand ourselves. However, this is where things have become confused. Although we are intimately aware that we are not zombies, certain worldviews, such as physicalism, imply otherwise.

Recently, I was watching a TV show called *The Walking Dead*. The plot is pretty simple: a disease has become rampant that can turn a person into a zombie, a walking, flesh-eating monster that lacks personhood. These zombies do not appear to be conscious. They can't communicate, can't be reasoned with, and they contain no hint of morality. They are a virus in human form, living out a mechanical existence of destruction. This disease is completely predictable; it walks around eating human flesh, like a terrifying form of flesh-eating disease.

There's an interesting scene in *The Walking Dead* where some survivors of this post-apocalyptic hell find refuge in a research facility. At one time, this was where scientists worked to find a cure. In a memorable speech, the last remaining researcher explains to the survivors the difference between a person and a zombie by showing them inside the brain of someone affected by the disease. Before the infection, there was a lightning storm of neurons inside the brain. After death, the entire brain shut down, only to "re-animate" with a lightning storm of neural activity in a different area of the brain. This was a zombie. As the scientist explains: "the frontal lobe, the neocortex, the human part... that doesn't come back. The you part. Just a shell driven by mindless instinct."[41]

So, what's the difference?

Where the lighting strikes.

Personhood requires only a slight difference in which neurons are firing. This is the implication of physicalism: we are nothing more than electrical activity in the brain. If that's the case, what is consciousness? The physicalist worldview can only say that it is just an illusion, that we are nothing more than our brain states, confused lighting storms of neural activity. In our culture today, it's not only God's existence that's being questioned, but also our very own. Do *you* exist?

Remember that earlier we talked about asking too much of science? Now, we are beginning to see the implications of a worldview that is limited to only *how* questions. Physicalism not only denies God's existence but also implicitly denies our own existence. Suddenly, we have become what we fear—the walking dead.

More than a Brain

Physicalism's approach to thinking about personhood just doesn't hold up to scrutiny. Plenty of scientific evidence and common sense suggests that we are more than three pounds of electrified grey matter.[42] Wilder Penfield, a famous neurosurgeon, used to probe the brains of patients who were awake. He could cause their bodies to do any number of things, including move their limbs and speak, yet Penfield says, "There is no place...where electrical stimulation will cause a patient to believe or to decide."[43] Likewise, even though stimulating the brain could cause a patient to speak, the patient remained stubbornly aware that it was Penfield who had made them speak, not themselves. How could this be possible if everything, even our consciousness, arises from the brain alone? If that were the case, we should be able to manipulate consciousness, yet we can't. In order to explain this, scientism is tempted to explain consciousness away as simply an illusion. However, this only raises the question: if consciousness is an illusion, then what is it that allows us to be aware of the illusion? Is our awareness of the illusion *another* illusion?

Further, if our personhood is nothing but the result of our brain and our DNA, then we should be able to divide personhood. J.P. Moreland, a theologian and expert on the philosophy of mind, put it this way:

I can't be the same thing as my body or brain. There was a story on television about an epileptic who underwent an operation in which surgeons removed fifty-three percent of her brain. When she woke up, nobody said, 'We have forty-seven percent of a person here.' A person can't be divided into pieces. You are either a person or you're not. But your brain and your body can be divided. So that means I can't be the same thing as my body.[44]

But, for a moment, let's just imagine what the world would be like if physicalism is true and everything is reducible to the purely physical. The implications of this kind of thinking are severe. It means that life is like a game of billiards. In a game of pool, every time you hit the cue ball, you can predict exactly where each ball will go, if you calculate the angles and velocity correctly. How is the universe any different? The particles that make up a person are just billiard balls set in motion by the Big Bang, which if calculated correctly, could be perfectly understood.

This would mean that you don't have free will. You are just particles of DNA, reacting to the world around you, the implications being that everything is coded for. Of course, this means that the bombing of the Boston Marathon was also coded for, not only in the perpetrators' DNA, but also in the Big Bang itself. Like billiard balls, those brothers couldn't have done otherwise—it was just physics.

If this is correct, then how can a collection of particles be held accountable? It's not their fault. They were just following their trajectory. Jails would become more like zoos, their only purpose being to keep dangerous animals away from others, rather than to punish evil behavior. The idea of punishing a wrong would become meaningless. Speaking of meaning, how can there be any? Meaning too becomes an illusion. The idea that we are only particles is a dangerous way of thinking. It's always interested me that when we watch zombie shows, we tend not to react to a zombie being killed. The first time I saw The Walking Dead on TV, I watched a police officer raise a large firearm and shoot a child, point-blank, in the head. The scene was horrendous, yet I didn't even wince at the little girl's execution. Why? She was a zombie.

Seriously, what's the difference between shooting a bag of chemicals and a zombie? Nothing, except that one is trying to eat you! It's significant that often in history when humans have committed grievous acts towards each other, these acts have often been preceeded by a campaign of dehumanization. Hitler is well-known for doing this with the Jews. This was also the case during the slave trade in North America. Enslaving and killing an animal, or a zombie, is much easier than doing so to a fellow human being. For this reason, I define Zombie Culture as a worldview that leads to the dehumanization of people.

Although some people believe that the implications of scientism are true, they don't live as though they are. Everyone believes that the men who bombed the Boston Marathon were guilty of their actions. Besides wanting to know *how*, *who*, and *why*, we also desire justice. We all know that people are valuable and that we must stop dehumanization around the world! But on what grounds can this be done? Jesus Christ's life was all about restoring people's humanity. On what grounds did he do so? Jesus taught that people are valuable because they were created in the image of a God who loves us.

It's all about relationship.

Again, looking through the microscope has brought us to something non-physical and relational in nature. While the human brain may be the apparatus through which consciousness is achieved, our true self, our soul, transcends the physical world. I believe our humanity is a gift from above that cannot be taken away or removed. You have meaning, purpose, and value because God gave it to you, making you in his very image. Perhaps we don't live as though physicalism is true because deep down we know it's not true. We do exist and our desire for relationship is real because a relational God does exist.

Hey God!
Why is it Not More Obvious that You Exist?

As I weigh the evidence from the telescope and microscope, I am persuaded not only that God exists, but also that I exist! I see good reason to conclude that a personal God is the author of both the cosmos and myself.

Yet, exploring scientific evidence for God's existence does lead me to one question: why do we even need these arguments in the first place? If God exists, and if Jesus is correct that the meaning of life is relationship with God, then why doesn't he go out of his way to reveal himself?

Have you ever wondered why God doesn't just put a giant billboard in the sky saying, "Yes, I exist"? When I was a child, I often asked for something similar, though on a smaller scale. On multiple occasions, I remember lying awake in bed asking God to turn on the lights. This request was partly a result of laziness, but also of doubt. Just once, I hoped to see that light turn on. I promised that I would never ask again and that I would follow God faithfully after that.

He never did it.

Why not?

Søren Kierkegaard (1813–1855), a Danish theologian, wrote an interesting parable that wrestled with this question and proposed possible reasons for God's hiddenness. His inspiration was a love story in the Bible where King Solomon disguises himself as a shepherd in order to win the heart of a woman.

The parable says that a king fell in love with a peasant maiden. Being a good king, he did not wish to take her hand in marriage by force, but rather to win her authentic love. But how exactly could he, as the king, go about doing that?

Moreover, how would the King of Kings, God, go about doing that?

If the king were to enter her village with all of his power, wealth, and beauty, the poor maiden would be so seduced or terrified that she would be incapable of saying no to his proposal. Even if he raised her up to his level, she would always know that she was not his equal, and their love could not be true. As Kierkegaard says, "The unhappiness of this love does not come from the inability of the lovers to realize their union, but from their inability to understand one another."[45] The only way that their love could be truly complete, Kierkegaard hypothesizes, is if the king were to reduce himself, to come to the maiden in her lowly state and be like her.

God is the definition of power, wealth, and beauty. Like the king and the maiden, his presence would be beyond overwhelming— it would be crippling. How could you freely love a God whose beauty is beyond compare? How do you choose whether to love a God whose wealth is beyond measure? Or a God whose power is limitless?

It would seem that a certain level of distance is required from God in order for us to have a real relationship with him.[46] Could it be that the hiddenness of God is not in an effort to harm us, but rather is the work of a loving God who desires not to force our love, but to woo it? Just like the king and the maiden, the Bible says that God has gone out of his way to make his presence known in the most loving way possible: he lowered himself and became a man. The Apostle Paul tells us in Philippians 2:4-8,

> Each of you should look not only to your own interests, but also to the interests of others. Your attitude should be the same as that of Christ Jesus: Who, being in very nature God, did not consider equality with God something to be grasped, but made himself nothing, taking the very nature of a servant, being made in human likeness. And being found in appearance as a man, he humbled himself and became obedient to death – even death on a cross!

That's how much God loves you.

The truth is: God *has* made himself known. Looking out for your interests, the King of Kings became a servant to woo the love of his beloved—you! What more could God do than he has already done? Advertising his existence on a billboard wouldn't be loving; it would ruin us. Instead, he has left enough evidence behind to point us to him, if we only care to follow. Have you ever asked the opposite question: if God did not want to be known, why didn't he create the universe in such a way that we could neither look for nor find him? Yet, here we live in a universe that is leading straight to him, if we are willing to look. It leads me to believe not only that God exists, but also that he desires a relationship with us.

Conclusion

During my time at college, and since, I worked through many of my beliefs and doubts. I have firmly reached the conclusion that the universe only makes sense through the lens of a Christian worldview. As C.S. Lewis, a former atheist, declared, "I believe in Christianity as I believe that the sun has risen: not only because I see it, but because by it I see everything else."[47]

The best way I can describe my belief in God is with an example from my first wedding anniversary. My wife and I celebrated our first year of marriage by throwing ourselves out of a plane, which oddly enough, is also a similar experience to getting married. Before I plunged 10,000 feet to the earth with my beautiful wife, I had good reasons to trust that parachute. I had taken physics in high school. I understood how velocity and drag worked. I knew the facts. I even had eyewitness testimonies that said it worked. Yet, in the end, to truly know it, I still needed to jump out of that plane—which I did, with some rather high-pitched screaming. Asking my wife Nancy to marry me was a similar experience, albeit without the screaming. How did I know she loved me? I couldn't prove that she loved me, but I did have good reason to believe that she did.

Faith in God, according to Christianity, is no different. We can study the facts, of which there are many.[48] Yet, aside from facts, Jesus explains that we can also personally experience God. What's holding you back? It would seem that you have nothing to lose and everything to gain.

I can't prove with absolute certainty that God exists or that he loves me, but I have good reason to believe it. My confidence in that belief has grown these last 18 years since I first placed my trust in God and said yes to his offer of relationship. My relationship with God has changed my worldview, just like it changed my mom's. I not only see the world differently, but I also act differently in it.

I don't want to give the impression that following God is easy, but neither is jumping from a perfectly good airplane or getting married. It's difficult and there are times of doubt, fear, and frustration. But, that's normal. In moments of doubt, I encourage you to go back to the facts. Remind yourself of how you came to your belief. Most of all, I encourage you to place your trust in God. Seek to know God—he wants to know you! After all, he created you to be with him.

Perhaps you are convinced that God exists, but you're not sure who this God is. There are so many religions: how do we know which one is correct? Perhaps they all are? In the next chapter, we will examine the question, "Do all religions lead to God?"

THINKING?

Chapter Three

Do All Religions Lead to God?

Two years into our marriage, my wife and I had a crazy idea. Well, actually, I had a crazy idea and she listened. It's kind of a theme in the Steiger house. On this occasion, I suggested that we quit our jobs and travel the globe for a year. Nancy listened patiently and said, "*Sure*, that sounds wonderful..."

I don't think either of us thought it would actually happen. Yet, much to our surprise, a year later, we were driving to the airport. We had plane tickets in hand, one large backpack each, and about $40 a day to live on. During those twelve months, we traveled to eleven countries on an epic journey that had a profound impact on the way we understood the world and ourselves.

As you can imagine, we experienced a world full of cultures, beliefs, and practices that were very different from our own. In Northern Myanmar, we went on a trek through the beautiful hill country into some remote villages. In one village, our accommodation was in a small Buddhist monastery where a friendly monk greeted us. It felt like stepping back into time as the elderly monk took us on a tour of the village and introduced us to local families. At first, I was really impressed how the monk greeted the children by name. However, we found out later that when a child in the village is born, the parents bring the infant to the monastery and the monks name the baby. Apparently, this is a common practice in many areas of Myanmar.

In a little oasis in Egypt, near the Libyan border, we hired a local to take us on a sand boarding trip into the Great Sand Sea. After an awesome day of carving up the hot sand dunes, our Muslim guide invited us to his home for dinner. The meal was served on the floor with colorful pillows in a circle to recline on. Our host was very friendly, but to our surprise, his wife did not join us for dinner; instead, she ate in the kitchen with their children. He explained that, in order to eat, his wife needed to remove her burqa, a religious covering worn for modesty. Removing her burqa would reveal her face, something that was not permitted in front of a man who was not her husband. She ate in the kitchen in order that my wife and I could share a meal with her husband.

While traveling in India, my wife and I rafted for two days down the Ganges River, from its start in the Himalayan Mountains to the first city it reaches, Rishikesh. As we neared the city, we floated past the remains of a cremation in the water. On the shore, we could see the fires where dead bodies were being burned. As we landed on the banks of the city, we witnessed a family gathered around a deceased elderly woman who was being cremated. One of the girls on our trip stealthily got out her video camera and began to film. I was shocked that a person would want to film such a thing, and concerned about what the family's reaction might be. As I slowly backed away, a young man from the family spotted her. He reached out, grabbed her by the wrist, and pulled her closer to the fire, pushing people aside in the process. I thought he would be upset at her for imposing on their private family moment and treating it like a spectacle. However, to our surprise, he was merely helping her get a better view for filming! The young man was happy to share their traditions with us and explained how, after death, Hindus are ritually bathed in the Ganges River, openly burned on a pile of wood, and finally set adrift down the river.

Why do I share all of these stories?

I do so only to illustrate how our beliefs and perspectives on everything from birth, life, and death make up our worldview. As you can imagine, we all tend to assume that everyone sees the world the same way we do, but this only leads to confusion and miscommunication. It's easy to assume that all parents name their children, that every family entertains guests together around a dinner table, or that all people deal with the body of a departed loved one privately; however, for many around the world, these assumptions just aren't true.

For this reason, in my travels, I have learned to become a student of people. I have found that although you may know what a religion formally teaches, you never know exactly what an individual personally believes until you ask them. This is especially true considering how vastly nuanced each religion can be. The reality is, we all have slightly different perspectives that make our beliefs unique to us. Yet, we often continue to assume that everyone has similar beliefs to ourselves. A great example of this is the popular question: "Do all religions lead to God?"

The charitable nature of this question fits nicely into Western culture, where we've been taught that religious truth is a matter of perspective. However, this question actually reflects a significant level of religious ignorance in that it makes two major worldview assumptions: first, that all religions teach that God exists, and second, that the goal of all religions is to reach God. While these assumptions fit well with a Judeo-Christian worldview, a simple study into the world's religions reveals that these assumptions about reality are not shared.

Worldview Tour

To illustrate this, let's take a brief tour of the fundamental beliefs of the world's major worldviews. Throughout the tour, we will see that not all worldviews believe that God exists and we will notice that reaching God is not something that everyone agrees is possible or even desirable. Formally speaking, this is what the worldviews teach[1]:

Hinduism:

Hinduism teaches that there are many gods that are manifested in various forms and worshiped. However, behind all of these forms, there is really only one supreme reality called Brahman; although Brahman can be personified as different gods, they are still just an extension of this one reality. A Hindu priest explained the concept of Brahman to me using a bell. After repeatedly hitting a small bell, he explained that Brahman is like the sound waves that extend into all places. In Hinduism, people are called Atman and are also part of Brahman; it is famously said that Brahman is Atman and Atman is Brahman. In fact, in Hinduism, this is the human predicament: all are ignorant of their divine nature. Until they become aware of their unity with the divine, they are subject to the law of karma and stuck in the cycle of *samsara* (reincarnation) by being continually reborn after death. So, while it originally appears that Hinduism, with their many gods, ascribes to the first premise, that God exists, they see gods as only manifestations of an impersonal force, rather than individual beings, and thus, God doesn't really exist as a distinct personal entity.[2] In addition, Hinduism definitely does not hold to the second assumption of trying to reach God; rather, the goal of Hinduism is *moksha* (liberation) from the cycle of reincarnation, so as to merge into the oneness of Brahman, where the illusion of the distinct and unique self (the individual) disappears.

Buddhism:

Buddhism was founded by Siddhartha (563-483 BC), commonly known as the Buddha, who started with Hinduism and then reformed it. Strictly speaking, Buddhism does not teach that God exists. Buddhists believe that ultimate reality is an undifferentiated oneness or force. A monk once shared with me a helpful analogy that says the force is like the ocean. In this sea of oneness, persons or egos can develop like waves driven up by desire. As the desires grow, so too does the wave, creating the illusion of the individual as separate from the unifying force, which results in suffering. The goal of Buddhism is to end all desire in order that each individual wave will be stilled back into the calm of the oneness and all will cease to suffer. Therefore, the goal of Buddhism is not to reach God, but to reach a state of *nirvana*, a word meaning to extinguish or blow out (like a candle)—to cease to exist as a person.

Islam:

Islam holds to the first assumption, teaching that a personal God does exist, often referred to as Allah (the generic term for God in Arabic). Allah, however, is wholly Other, transcendent and unattainable, and therefore cannot be reached. Even the prophet, Muhammad (570-632 AD), needed an angel mediator in order to communicate with Allah. Allah's message to mankind is submission to the will of Allah. A Muslim is one who submits. After death, Islam teaches that all people will face judgment, where Allah will weigh their good and bad deeds and then decide their fates. The goal of Islam is to reach the afterlife, which is an earthly paradise full of pleasures. Yet, this earthly paradise, although near God, is not where Allah is; God is still wholly Other. Therefore, while Muslims ascribe to the first premise, that God exists, they do not hold to the second, that God can be reached.

Scientism:

While not a religion in the typical use of the word, Scientism does present an all-encompassing worldview with implications for every area of life. So in that sense, it functions the same way that religions do. Scientism does not hold to either premise about God; instead, it holds that ultimate reality is found only in the physical world. The goal of Scientism is to use empirical science to study the physical world. It is believed that, given enough time, science alone will be capable of answering all of life's questions about the universe and every aspect of human life because, ultimately, people are just particles in motion. Like Hinduism and Buddhism, Scientism teaches that personhood is ultimately an illusion and that, in death, the particles that made up the human body will just continue along their trajectory until eventually ceasing to exist in the heat death of the universe.

Judaism:

Judaism is a difficult religion to describe because of its long history and the many drastic changes that have been made to it over time. The current understanding of Judaism arose after the destruction of the temple in the year AD 70. With the abolishment of the entire sacrificial system, including the priesthood, a new form called Rabbinic Judaism arose, in which the rabbis gained the authority to establish Jewish laws and practices. Judaism underwent even more changes during the Enlightenment. Currently, there are three main branches of Judaism: Orthodox, Conservative, and Reform. Orthodox Judaism is the closest to the Old Testament Judaism from which Christianity has its roots. Orthodox Jews believe that God does exist and can be reached. However, the majority of Jews today fall into the other two categories. Conservative Judaism holds to an impersonal God that cannot be known. Reform Judaism tends to hold to a 'God concept' which is interpreted in many different ways and cannot be reached. However, some believe in an impersonal force that souls can merge into. For many Jews today, their Jewishness is more an ethnic and cultural heritage than a system of belief, and many modern Jews are either atheist or agnostic.[3]

Christianity:

Christianity is a continuation or fulfillment of Old Testament Judaism. It teaches that one God exists in three persons: Father, Son, and Holy Spirit. Christians believe that Jesus is the Son of God and the Messiah that many Old Testament Jews were waiting for. Jesus, specifically through his death on the cross, saves people from God's judgment and, thus, provides the way for followers to have a right relationship with God through faith. Christianity teaches that God has reached out to people, through Christ, and the result is that believers can live forever with God in a new heaven and a new earth.

As you can see, the question, "Do all religions lead to God?" is actually an attempt to impose one worldview onto another. In fact, outside of the Judeo-Christian worldview, I do not know of another religion that teaches both that a personal God exists and also that you can personally reach God. The question that really should be asked is this: "Are all religions true?"

Which, if any, of these worldviews is correct?

Religions are not just seeking to add their own interesting perspectives to the world. Rather, all religions are making truth claims—claims about the way the world *really is*. That being the case, it's easy to see that the world's religions can't all be true. What if I were to make up a religion? Would it suddenly become true? And what about religions that are contradictory, as most of them are? Can they *all* be correct? Can God both exist and not exist at the same time? Can God both be reached and not reached? Which is it? Or are they all wrong?

Climbing Truth Mountain

Claiming that all religions are correct, or that they teach the same thing, is to not take them seriously, nor to understand what they actually teach. Christianity is infamously accused of being arrogant and exclusive of other religions, claiming not only to *be* true, but also to be the *only* truth. However, it's important to understand that it isn't Christianity that is exclusive—it's truth itself. By its very nature, truth excludes everything false. Think about it. Simply disagreeing with that statement proves the point: even the person who says "there is no truth" seems to believe that *it's true* that there is no truth! You just can't get away from it—truth is exclusive and every religion claims to be true.

Many people want to deny the exclusivity of truth and claim instead that all religions are equally true, an idea often called religious pluralism. One common approach is to use an analogy that describes life as climbing a mountain. It's suggested that we are all on different paths heading up to the same summit. Along the way, we may see different views and landscapes depending on which "trail" we are following, but in the end we will all reach the same destination.

At first glance this analogy sounds nice, doesn't it? I mean, it sounds so tolerant and inclusive of everyone, which is something that western culture strives for.

However, what may appear to show a harmony of competing worldviews, upon closer examination, actually proves the exclusive nature of truth.

The story implies that all of the world's religions have only part of the truth about reality, the part that their side of the mountain reveals. Only someone with a greater vantage point, someone completely off of the mountain, can see the whole picture and know the whole truth. So, who is claiming that greater vantage point? The person claiming that all religions are true! It raises the question: how did they get off the mountain? How can they see the whole truth when everyone else can't? You see, rather than denying exclusive truth, this illustration only confirms it by claiming that religious pluralism is the exclusive truth!

In that sense, the belief that all religions lead to the same destination is no different than the beliefs of other religions. It is a truth claim—a claim to have the greater vantage point and to see reality correctly. However, the problem with a belief in religious pluralism is that in order for it to be true, the world's religions all must believe in something fundamentally similar. At the very least, they have to believe in the mountain and in the goal to reach the top. Yet, as we've already discussed, the world's religions are vastly different from one another. What of the Buddhist or Atheist who doesn't believe in the mountain in the first place? Or what of the Hindu, who doesn't want to reach the top of the mountain, but rather escape the mountain entirely? Or the Muslim who believes the summit is unreachable and instead strives for an oasis near the top?

The basic rules of logic tell us that contradictory statements cannot both be true in the same sense and at the same time—this is how the law of non-contradiction works. It seems self-evident that it is impossible for God to both exist and not-exist at the same time. Ultimate reality cannot be both an impersonal force and a personal being at the same time. Common sense dictates that either we are both wrong or only one of us is right. Because the world's religions disagree at such a fundamental level, it's just not logically possible that they are *all* true. We cannot all be on the same mountain.

I once was speaking with a Pure Land Buddhist monk about this. I knew that Pure Land Buddhism (Mahayana Buddhism) disagreed with certain aspects of Tibetan Buddhism (Tantra Buddhism). Mahayana Buddhism takes certain Buddhist teachings, such as that of the Hungry Ghost, as metaphor, whereas Tantra Buddhism interprets teachings more literally. So, I asked the monk if he thought that both approaches were right. In response, the monk acknowledged that it was logically impossible for them both to be correct; however, he was able to harmonize the two competing beliefs with some logical sleight-of-hand. The monk concluded that Tibetan Buddhists were merely practicing Pure Land Buddhism in ignorance.

We might smirk at his answer, but isn't that what the mountain analogy is really suggesting? Basically, the monk was saying that we are all climbing the mountain of Mahayana Buddhism, we just don't know it yet. Notice, however, that the monk did not think he was climbing the mountain of Tantra Buddhism and was merely ignorant of it. If he did, he would have changed his belief.

That's the problem with climbing the religious mountain. We all believe we have the true perspective. If we didn't, we would change our belief about the mountain. In other words: we don't see ourselves as the ones climbing the mountain, but as the ones telling the story. It's *our* truth that everyone else is ignorantly climbing. If you press the mountain analogy to its logical conclusion, it implies that everyone except you is wrong.

True For Me

What about people that say, "Your religion is true for you and my religion is true for me?" After all, this has become the religious slogan of the postmodern era.

I must confess that it sounds nice. I think a statement like this often stems from a sincere desire to get along with each other; in our culture, it seems rude and judgmental to call someone's beliefs wrong. However, in this case, politeness and acceptance have been taken too far and the result is just nonsense. The statement that "it's true for me" implies a belief that sincerity is all that is required for a belief to be true; if we believe in something with all our heart, then that's good enough.

The problem is: we would never entertain this idea with anything else. Imagine if a criminal claimed in court that, "Your law is true for you and my law is true for me." No one would consider that a valid argument! Oxford theologian Michael Green provides additional examples. He says:

They would never say it about a historical topic like World War Two: you may sincerely believe Hitler won, but you would be mistaken. They would never apply it to mathematics: nobody in their right mind imagines that if only they believe hard enough that two and two equals five, that would make it so...No, it is only in the area of religion that people talk like this, perhaps because it is so hard to achieve certainty in religion. The topic is as slippery as soap in water. Much better, then, to duck out of the subject altogether and airily suggest that it does not matter what you believe as long as you are sincere.[4]

So, if it is so obvious that sincerity is not a valid source of truth, then what is going on here?

Why do people continue to claim that their beliefs are "true for them?"

I suggest that what has happened is merely a word swap. Our culture has substituted the word "true" for the word "meaningful." What we really should be saying is, "Your religion is meaningful to you and my religion is meaningful to me." After all, I think we would all agree that religions, even made up ones, are meaningful to those that practice them.

The problem is, religions aren't claiming to be meaningful—they're claiming to be true.

True For Everyone

The importance of truth suddenly becomes crystal clear when our life is on the line. This was the case for me several years ago, when I went bungee jumping for the first time off of a bridge in Whistler, BC. Honestly, I'm not sure why people pay money to flirt with gravity. I did, and it was terrifying.

I went with a group of friends, and so I tried to remain manly as I mustered the courage to throw myself off of a bridge. With only a small cord attached to my legs, I was obviously concerned for my safety as I started inching my way toward the 160-foot drop. On the drive up, I had imagined myself confidently strutting to the ledge and springing off into a perfect swan dive, arms spread out wide, the wind blowing across my body as I gracefully flew through the air.

The reality was much different.

I quickly realized that it would take all the courage I could muster just to fall off the platform, into the fetal position, while screaming at the top of my lungs! Taking some deep breaths, I turned to the guy who had just strapped me in. With sweaty palms, weak knees, and a lump in my throat, I asked, "Did you properly attach the bungee cord to my legs? Is it secure?"

Now, I promise you: I was *not* looking for just a meaningful answer, nor was the question open to interpretation. I wanted the truth. I knew that within a couple of seconds, I would be confronted with reality. My life depended on it.

Religion is no different and the stakes are just as high.

All religions are making truth claims, and the importance of those claims is life or death. I think that's why this question is so important to us. We recognize the importance of truth and also the reality that so many people disagree with each other. The thought of so many people being wrong has led some people to get even more creative in attempting to harmonize the world's religions. They suggest that the world's religions may only *appear* to be contradictory. Could it be that religions only disagree on the surface, and upon deeper investigation, they turn out to actually be different descriptions of the same reality?

Elephant in the Room

A popular illustration of the attempted harmonization of religion is the Hindu parable of the blind men and the elephant. This analogy seeks to demonstrate that the world's religions merely appear to be in contradiction, and claims that they actually speak of a singular reality.

Although told in slightly different ways, the parable goes something like this: three blind men approach an elephant and begin touching it in order to discern what it is. The first blind man feels the trunk and describes it as a palm tree. The second blind man feels the tail and describes it as a rope. The third blind man feels the ear and describes it as a fan. Only the storyteller, who is not blind, can see that they are each describing the same object, the elephant, each from his own unique perspective. It is suggested that each religion does the same.

Like the previous analogy of the mountain, this parable is seriously flawed and in much the same way; instead of making truth relative, the parable of the blind men and the elephant is actually a great example of the exclusive nature of truth and highlights wonderfully the fundamental flaw of all religions.

First, in the same way that the analogy of the mountain assumed that religious pluralists can see the truth while the religious faithful can't, this parable also has a storyteller who has the privileged position of seeing the truth—that the blind men are all touching the same thing. To point out the issue with this idea, Christian thinker Greg Koukl suggests asking the person promoting the analogy a simple question. He says:

> Ask, 'Where would you be in the illustration? When you apply this parable to the issue of truth, are you like one of the blind men or are you like the [story-teller]?' This dilemma is unsolvable. If the story-teller is like one who can't see—if he is one of the blind men groping around— how does he know everyone else is blind and has only a portion of the truth? On the other hand, if he fancies himself in the position of the [story-teller], how is it that he alone escapes the illusion that blinds the rest of us?[5]

You see, by exempting itself from blindness, religious pluralism asserts the existence of objective truth; it claims that pluralism alone can correctly understand reality.

Second, despite being used as an illustration to show how all religions are simultaneously true, the parable ends up showing the opposite. After all, the blind men weren't all right, they were all absolutely mistaken; it's not a palm tree, or a rope, or a fan— it's an elephant! They weren't even close to being correct! Thus, the parable doesn't prove that all religions are correct. Rather, the best it can do is try to demonstrate that all religions, except pluralism, are wrong.

Lastly, it's important to note that both this parable and the story of the mountain don't *prove* anything anyway. Professor of Philosophy Paul Copan explains this well:

> One problem with this mountaintop (or elephant and blind-men) analogy is that analogies don't *prove* a point, they only *illustrate* it. While analogies may be powerful, they may only illustrate false, misleading ideas...Let's switch the analogy. If Jesus is truly unique, maybe the world's religions are like a maze or labyrinth with one way out; what if God in Christ steps into this maze to help us walk through it?[6]

Does this analogy of the maze *prove* the validity of the Christian faith? Of course not. It may provide a helpful way of understanding an argument, but it should not be confused for the argument itself. In order to test the reasonableness of any belief, we need to look for other evidence outside of analogy.

Born Blind

Now, I actually think that the parable of the blind men and the elephant is helpful, but not in the way it is normally used. Remember that all the men in the parable were blind and described reality incorrectly; they were just groping for truth from their limited understanding. This is a great illustration of the fundamental problem of religion: we are all born blind to the truth.

Have you ever considered that if God exists that he would be, by nature, unreachable? Think about it. How do you expect to reach God unless God first wants to be reached? In fact, if you think God is someone that you can reach purely through your own effort, perhaps you need to rethink just how big your view of God is!

I am convinced that if God did not want to be reached, we would never reach God. More than that, we wouldn't even think about God. As discussed in chapter two, the facts that we can think about God and that the world is intelligible seem like good indications that God wants to be reached.

But if God wants to be reached, *he* needs to be the one to initiate.

How do we, the created, ever expect to be able to reach the creator unless he first makes a way or gives us sight?

Are we not like the blind men in comparison to God?

This brings us back again to Jesus' answer to the meaning of life. If God created us for the purpose of relationship with himself, it raises the question of how God is seeking to facilitate that relationship in light of our blindness. This is where Christianity's answer to the question "Do all religions lead to God?" is helpful and begins to point us in the right direction.

The answer to the question, "Do all religions lead to God?" is a firm *no*—in fact, they're not even trying. But, then again, Christianity teaches that *no* religion leads to God. Michael Green says it this way:

> What we need is not to compare the chinks of light that different religions may have perceived, but to experience the sunrise, which eclipses the light of every candle. We do not need a religion, but a revelation. And that is precisely what Christianity claims to be. Unlike other holy books, the Bible does not record the story of human beings in search of God, but of God in search of human beings.[7]

Christianity teaches that although it's impossible to work your way to God, God can and did work his way to you. Jesus did not present a religious way to reach God—that's the blind man's approach. Instead, he claimed to be God in the flesh; the storyteller became a character in the story.

Unique

When you read the Gospels (Matthew, Mark, Luke, and John), the Bible's four accounts of Jesus' life, you find that Jesus was unlike anyone in history. He spoke with a unique kind of authority. Matthew 7:28-29 says, "When Jesus had finished saying these things, the crowds were amazed at his teaching, because he taught as one who had authority, and not as their teachers of the law." Everyone immediately knew that Jesus wasn't just a messenger from God like other prophets.

Jesus spoke as the author.

It's important to note that Jesus didn't claim to have discovered the way to God; he claimed to *be* the way. He did not claim to have learned the truth about God; he claimed to *be* truth. He did not claim to have found life; he claimed to *be* life. These claims naturally exclude all other religious ideas. As Jesus declared in John 14:6, "I am the way and the truth and the life. No one comes to the Father except through me."

People may find Jesus' exclusive statements arrogant, but aren't we searching for the truth? Jesus taught that God is too great to be reached and that is why all of the world's religions fail—they are man's attempt to reach God. Rather, Christianity is about how the all-knowing reached the unknowing; how the seeing came alongside the blind; how ultimate reality, God himself, has reached us in a person.

This idea is so radical that many have questioned whether we have understood Jesus correctly. I mean, did Jesus really claim to *be* ultimate reality—God himself?

A '78 Dodge Colt and a Jehovah's Witness

I can still remember sitting at the bus stop, holding a new alternator for my '78 Dodge Colt. I was waiting for a bus that would take me back to my college campus, where my broken car was awaiting repair. The irony of the situation was that I was about to learn that I too was in need of some fixing up. As with most things in my life, I would learn the hard way.

That day at the bus stop was the first time in my life that my beliefs about God were openly challenged. While waiting for the bus, a man came up to me and asked passionately if I would like to know Jesus Christ. Considering that I was a Christian and in my second year of Bible college, I figured this would be a pleasant exchange.

I was wrong.

Wanting to impress him, I started to tell him exactly how well I knew Jesus. It didn't go well. He became physically upset by my response. The veins on his neck and forehead looked ready to burst as he raised his voice and asked again, "Do you want to know Jesus?" At this point, I figured I must have done a poor job of explaining myself. So this time, I unleashed my full theological arsenal.

This only made matters worse. The man's frustrated ranting became so animated that it was starting to draw a crowd around us. I am sure they were all expecting a fight to break out at any minute. Meanwhile, I was completely confused as to why this guy was so upset. I finally asked him what was wrong. It turned out that he was a Jehovah's Witness and was upset that I kept referring to Jesus as God.[8] In the middle of our bus stop fight circle, which was pretty large by this time, he waved a Bible at me and asked, "Where in the Bible does Jesus say, 'I am God'?"

I had no answer for him.

What followed next could only be described as a public spanking with a Bible! I couldn't defend one of the foundational beliefs of Christianity and the keystone of my life—that Jesus was God in the flesh.

When the bus dropped me off at campus later that day, I can honestly say that it was like arriving at college for the first time. I was now a student. Realizing the depths of my ignorance, I wanted to know why I believed Jesus was God, and whether I should continue to believe it.

I Am

It might surprise you to learn that Jesus never did say the exact words, "I am God." True, the authors of the Bible refer to Jesus as God many times,[9] but if Jesus directly made this claim about himself, then that's a different story. The fact that those exact words aren't in the Bible frustrates many people. I mean, it does seem like a lot of confusion would have been avoided.

Well, it turns out that only we in the twenty-first century are confused. The first century Jews that listened and followed Jesus understood exactly who he claimed to be. They were not confused because he spoke of God in the way they understood.

One of the greatest hurdles we have in understanding the Bible is our tendency to read it as a twenty-first century document. Doing so leads us to ask inappropriate questions and to take everything wildly out of context.

Consider this: if Jesus wanted to say "I am God," exactly how would he have done that?

It seems like a simple question, but remember what language the Gospels were written in. They were written in Greek, but Jesus was most likely speaking Aramaic, a language in the same sub-family as Hebrew. Now consider, what was the Hebrew name for the God of Israel? The only personal name for the God of Israel in Hebrew is YHWH.

When you read that, did you pronounce it in your mind?

If you've seen YHWH before, you might have pronounced it "Yahweh," but that's only because in recent times we have added in the missing vowels.[10] In its written form, Biblical Hebrew did not use vowels for the entire written language, they simply remembered where the vowels should go and pronounced it accordingly when they read. However, among all of Hebrew, the word YHWH was unique. In that word alone, the Jews did not add any vowels, ever. This is because, out of reverence for God and to avoid misusing God's name, it was purposely kept unpronounceable. When they read text where YHWH was present, they would read the word *Adonai* meaning "Lord" instead.[11] Although we have created a way to pronounce the name of the Hebrew God, no first century Jew could say it; they could only write it. Therefore, Jesus just literally couldn't *say* "I am YHWH."

That being the case, why couldn't Jesus have used the Greek word *theos* (God) or the generic Hebrew word *El* (God)? The problem is similar to the problem in English, where the word "God" isn't specific and can be used for any and all gods. In the first century, people believed in all sorts of gods, all of which could have been described by *theos* or *El*. Thus, had Jesus used those words for himself, the people, Jew and Gentile alike, would have responded, "Which god are you claiming to be?" Jesus didn't want to confuse them by claiming to be just any god. He wanted to tell everyone that he was the God of Israel, and so he did it the only way that was possible.

It's something that we do all the time. Consider how you talk about a person whose name you cannot pronounce or remember. You describe them. This is exactly what the Jews did when they spoke of YHWH—they spoke of YHWH's attributes. For example, when I saw my wife for the first time, at a school Christmas party, I failed to learn her name. So, the next day, I described her to my roommates. I said, "Remember that girl in the red dress? She was sitting at the table beside you. She's about 5'8, has green eyes, long brown hair, and is absolutely gorgeous!" They all knew exactly who I was talking about.

In the same way, the Jews understood exactly who Jesus was claiming to be because he described himself as YHWH. In fact, the 'nicknames' for God in the Old Testament are derived from YHWH's attributes; they are descriptions. The name *El Shaddai* emphasizes that he is the Almighty One or all-powerful. The name *El Olam* indicates that he is the Everlasting One or eternal. Even at the burning bush, when God reveals his name to Moses, he says, "I Am that I Am."[12] YHWH used the verb *to be* or *to exist*, "I Am," as his name. This is the attribute of aseity or self-existence. Basically YHWH was telling Moses to go tell Pharaoh that the self-existent one had sent him. Pharaoh would know exactly who that was.

I find it interesting that when YHWH is described by his attributes like this, it transcends culture and language. We all understand who is meant by the all-powerful, eternal, and self-existent one.

The God of Gods. The King of Kings.

Blasphemy

Throughout the Gospels, Jesus asserted his own divinity by continually claiming, for himself, the attributes of God. A good example of this is found in Mark 2. Jesus is teaching in a home crowded with people when a group of men who are desperate to reach Jesus cut a hole in the roof and lower a paralyzed man before Jesus to be healed. To the amazement of the crowd, Jesus looks at the man and says, "Son, your sins are forgiven." We then read: "now some teachers of the law were sitting there, thinking to themselves, 'Why does this fellow talk like that? He's blaspheming! Who can forgive sins but God alone?'"[13]

You see the Jews understood that even though Jesus did not say, "I am God," he was describing himself as God. There were only two choices: either Jesus was God and was telling the truth about himself, or he was committing the crime of blasphemy, making oneself equal with God, punishable by death. The passage continues:

> Immediately Jesus knew in his spirit that this was what
> they were thinking in their hearts, and he said to them,
> "Why are you thinking these things? Which is easier: to
> say to this paralyzed man, 'Your sins are forgiven,' or to

say, 'Get up, take your mat and walk'? But I want you to know that the Son of Man has authority on earth to forgive sins." So he said to the man, "I tell you, get up, take your mat and go home." He got up, took his mat and walked out in full view of them all. This amazed everyone and they praised God, saying, "We have never seen anything like this!"[14]

The Jews understood that only God could forgive sins, and he did so once a year on the Day of Atonement (*Yom Kippur*) in the innermost part of the temple, the Holy of Holies, where only the high priest could enter. This was a significant sacrificial event that only the high priest could perform on behalf of the people. Now, in that context, imagine how mind-bending it was for Jesus to forgive a man's sin in an average house, without a sacrifice, and most importantly, using his own authority! Anyone committing blasphemy like that should have been struck down by God right then and there. You get the sense that those present are beginning to slowly back away from Jesus. Yet, instead of God zapping this blasphemer on the spot, he shows Jesus honor! God shows that he supports Jesus' claim to divinity by immediately allowing him to physically heal the paralyzed man! Something like this had never been seen before, and it shattered everyone's expectations. As you can imagine, those who encountered Jesus often left with a lot to think about.

Death Penalty

Let's consider one more passage from Mark 14, when Jesus is arrested and put on trial. Caiaphas, the Jewish high priest, has an important dialogue with Jesus. He asks Jesus, "Are you the Messiah, the Son of the Blessed One?"[15]

Notice what just happened.

Caiaphas really wants to ask Jesus the same question we all want to ask, whether Jesus is claiming to be God, but he can't because he can't speak God's name. Instead, he asks the question by using a description, "the Blessed One." Jesus' response is significant. He says, "I AM, and you will see the Son of Man sitting at the right hand of the Mighty One and coming on the clouds of heaven."[16]

Jesus is saying more than just "yes" when he says "I AM." This is the same verb *to exist* that God used as his own name to Moses at the burning bush. In fact, many believe that this is where the name YHWH comes from; it is a form of the verb *to exist* in Hebrew. So, imagine what Caiaphas heard when Jesus said that? Remember, these Jews knew their scriptures backwards and forwards. They knew without a doubt that Jesus was claiming to be the same God who spoke to Abraham and Moses.[17]

As if that wasn't clear enough, Jesus immediately continues on by claiming that a prophecy of God's coming judgment and rule, found in Daniel 7:13 and Psalm 110:1, is actually about himself. Again, Caiaphas wouldn't have misunderstood. As Jesus was speaking, Caiaphas would have interpreted Jesus' words as something like, "currently, you are judging me, Caiaphas, but I am the King and soon a day is coming when I will judge you."

Jesus was laying claim to more attributes of God, this time his role as Judge and Ruler. Caiaphas got the message and responded as follows:

> The high priest tore his clothes. "Why do we need any more witnesses?" he asked. "You have heard the blasphemy. What do you think?" They all condemned him as worthy of death. Then some began to spit at him; they blindfolded him, struck him with their fists, and said, "Prophesy!" And the guards took him and beat him.[18]

Notice that Caiaphas sentenced Jesus to death for claiming to be God, and Jesus willingly accepted that judgment.

Conclusion

It's interesting that the Jews wanted to kill Jesus not for what he taught or did, but for who he claimed to be. This is because speaking with the voice of God is putting yourself in the ultimate place of authority; it is claiming the narrator's or storyteller's perspective and it still upsets people to this day. Jesus was claiming to see reality—all of reality—correctly.

Christianity is unique in that it is not about a way of life; fundamentally, it's about a person. Christians are obsessed with Jesus because he claimed to be the author or narrator. Everything hinges on Jesus: was he who he claimed to be?

That's a question that we'll address in a later chapter. For now, let's consider: if he is the narrator, then what did Jesus say was the truth? What was Jesus' worldview?

First, Jesus made it very clear that all religions can't lead to God. Rather, he said that he alone is the way to salvation because, through him, God reached us.

Jesus did not describe a world in which we are all climbing the same mountain, but rather he said we are all descending from the same purpose. The Bible began with people living in relationship with God; Adam and Eve were living for the purpose they were created for until evil entered the world and separated all of mankind from God. Essentially, we started at the top of the mountain and have been falling ever since.

Likewise, Jesus did not describe a world full of blind people who each grasp at their portion of the truth, but a world of spiritually dead people in rebellion against God. The effect of physical death is separation from people, but the effect of spiritual death is separation from God. This is humanity's greatest need and God's most urgent concern. It is also the thing that makes Christianity unique among faiths. Christian thinker Ravi Zacharias says it like this:

> But the question arises as to what makes the Christian framework unique. Here we see the second cardinal difference between the Judeo-Christian worldview and the others. It is simply this: no amount of moral capacity can get us back into a right relationship with God... Herein lies the cardinal difference between the moralizing religions and Jesus' offer to us. Jesus does not offer to make bad people good but to make dead people alive.[19]

Jesus' mission is to bring us life.

This is true for all people. Jesus loves the broken, whether a prostitute or a thief. The self-righteous religious leaders made Jesus incredibly frustrated, yet he loved them too. Jesus loves all people and desires that everyone come into relationship with himself. The Apostle Paul says it like this in 1 Timothy 2:3-6a:

> This is good, and pleases God our savior, who wants all people to be saved and to come to a knowledge of the truth. For there is one God and one mediator between God and mankind, the man Christ Jesus, who gave himself as a ransom for all people.

Jesus makes it very clear that God loves us and wants to be in relationship with us.

Yet, this doesn't seem to match reality.

If God wants to be in relationship with everyone, then why isn't he? If he wants to love everyone, then why is there evil?

The comedian George Carlin amusingly gets at the heart of the dilemma saying:

> When it comes to believing in God, I really tried. I really, really, tried. I tried to believe that there is a God, who created each of us in his own image and likeness, loves us very much, and keeps a close eye on things. I really tried to believe that, but I gotta tell you, the longer you live, the more you look around, the more you realize...something is wrong here. War, disease, death, destruction, hunger, filth, poverty, torture, crime, corruption, and the Ice Capades. Something is definitely wrong. This is not good work. If this is the

best God can do, I am not impressed. Results like these do not belong on the resume of a Supreme Being. This is the kind of [stuff] you'd expect from an office temp with a bad attitude.[20]

Many people agree with him. They may agree that not all religions lead to God, but they don't like the type of God that Christianity leads us towards. That's why any discussion of Jesus' worldview will, at some point, lead you to ask the question of the next chapter, "Why is there evil?"

THINKING?

Chapter Four

Why is There Evil?

During the year that my wife and I traveled the globe, we made sure that one of our stops was in Calcutta, India. Mother Teresa (1910-1997) and her mission made the poverty in Calcutta well-known throughout the world. Although I knew that the poverty would be severe, I looked forward to helping in any way that I could.

We ended up spending the month of December, including Christmas, serving with Mother Teresa's Missionaries of Charity in both the Kalighat hospice (Home of the Dying) and at an orphanage. Mother Teresa started Kalighat in order to love and care for impoverished and destitute people during their last few days of life. It is meant to give people from the street a place where they can die in dignity. This ministry eventually gave birth to many other ministries, such as the orphanage where I also worked.

On my second day, I was serving at the orphanage when a little boy was brought in from the street. He looked about two years old and had been found in some bushes at the local train station. Since no one knew him and he couldn't speak, it was decided that he would be called Raju. From the moment that I first walked into his room, my heart absolutely broke. There he was, sitting on the floor, alone and obviously terrified. Even from across the room, I could see that Raju was blind. His beautiful eyes had white cataracts that slightly protruded from his dark brown pupils. Raju hadn't been born blind; rather, his blindness had been caused by severe poverty and the detrimental effects of long-term malnourishment. I'll never forget scooping him up into my arms for the first time. I was overwhelmed with sorrow and anger. More than anything, I wished that I could smuggle him away to safety.

As I held Raju, he started to cry and so did I. It wasn't until I started to speak softly to him that he finally settled down. Hearing someone's voice was like a light in his darkness and it calmed his fears, letting him know that he wasn't alone and that it was going to be okay. Yet, as I held Raju, I must confess: I didn't feel like it was going to be okay. I had never met anyone more impoverished than him. He literally had nothing and no one. His poverty had even robbed him of his sight. What kind of future did this little blind boy have?

Mother Teresa's journal is full of stories of pain and suffering like Raju's. To many, her life appears so saint-like that it is tempting to assume that her relationship with God made her impervious to the effects of evil. The reality is that she struggled with the problem of evil the same way that many of us do. One writer described her life by saying:

Soon after [Mother Teresa] left the convent and began her work among the destitute and dying on the street, the visions and locutions ceased, and she experienced a spiritual darkness that would remain with her until her death... she disclosed feelings of doubt, loneliness, and abandonment. God seemed absent, heaven empty, and bitterest of all, her own suffering seemed to count for nothing, "...just that terrible pain of loss, of God not wanting me, of God not being God, of God not really existing."[1]

Mother Teresa's struggle with the problem of evil was a similar struggle to the one that faced Reaksa Himm, a man I had the privilege of spending a week with in 2013. Over the course of our time together, Reaksa told me his heart-wrenching story; it's a story that displays the depths of human depravity.

Reaksa Himm grew up in Cambodia during the time of the Khmer Rouge, a communist party led by Pol Pot that was responsible for the deaths of millions of Cambodians. The Himm family were forced from their home and trapped in a series of small jungle villages where they lived and labored, half-starved and in constant fear of the local Khmer leaders who might execute them without warning. Then, when he was fourteen, Reaksa was arrested, along with his parents, brothers, and sisters, and taken to the killing fields to be executed. In his book, *The Tears of My Soul*, Reaska writes:

My father was standing and facing the grave. They kicked his legs from behind so he fell onto his knees; as he turned his head to look at me I saw them club him with a hoe. He fell forward into the grave with a scream...Then it was our turn. They made us kneel in front of the grave, and as I knelt I felt a blow on my neck and fell into the grave on top of my father. He was still alive, and I heard his last few breaths. Then there was nothing. My younger brothers and sisters and the other children tumbled into the grave too, on top of me. Finally, they clubbed my baby brother. The first three times they clubbed him he screamed loudly, then they clubbed him one more time and I didn't hear him again.[2]

Reaksa's entire family were brutally murdered and pushed into a mass grave. Yet, miraculously, the blow Reaksa received didn't kill him and he managed to escape. This was hardly an escape to freedom. Although Reaksa fled Cambodia and eventually came to live in Canada, he was tormented by the psychological trauma of experiencing such evil. For a long time, he would bear the emotional scars of that event and be filled with an anger that nearly consumed him. Before coming to Canada, he had met a group of Christians who tried to share God's love with him, but he writes:

> I wasn't interested...Buddhism hadn't helped me in my distress, so why should any other religion help me? I didn't want the lifeline of faith: I wanted to survive on my own. I didn't have time or energy for God; I didn't want to be led in his way. I preferred my own way, even though that meant anger, and helplessness, and misery. I closed my heart to everything they said. "If God is so good and powerful, why did he allow the Khmer Rouge to kill my family?" I would ask.[3]

Isn't that the question of the ages?

Haven't you ever felt like Mother Teresa did? Doesn't the pain of people like Reaksa Himm or Raju, as well as your own suffering, grieve your soul and make you cry out, "WHY?"

Everywhere we look in this world, evil is staring us in the face. A brief look at daily headlines reminds us of the poverty, violence, corruption, death, and despair throughout our world. None of us are immune. So, what does that mean about God?

After all, if God is all-powerful then he should be able to eliminate evil and if God is all-good then he should want to eliminate it. Yet, here we are in a world full of evil. Doesn't this mean that an all-powerful, all-good God can't possibly exist?

I Believe in Evil

This is the conclusion that many people have come to. Recently, a close friend told me how his brother, having just come back from humanitarian work in Africa, had given up on God. The evil he witnessed in Africa had caused him to lose faith and, ultimately, hope. He just could not reconcile the evil he had witnessed with an all-good and all-powerful author who loved and cared for his creation.

Bart Ehrman, a well-known former Christian turned skeptic, lost his faith in a similar way. He says:

> The problem of suffering became for me the problem of faith. After many years of grappling with the problem, trying to explain it, thinking through the explanations that others have offered—some of them pat answers charming for their simplicity, others highly sophisticated and nuanced reflections of serious philosophers and theologians—after thinking about the alleged answers

and continuing to wrestle with the problem, about nine or ten years ago I finally admitted defeat, came to realize that I could no longer believe in the God of my tradition, and acknowledged that I was an agnostic: I don't "know" if there is a God; but I think that if there is one, he certainly isn't the one proclaimed by the Judeo-Christian tradition, the one who is actively and powerfully involved in this world. And so I stopped going to church.[4]

Yet, what's interesting about Ehrman is that his wife, an intelligent and acclaimed academic in her own right, remains a committed Christian. Ehrman writes, "For her the problems of suffering that I wrestle with are not problems. It's funny how smart and well-meaning people can see things so differently, even on the most basic and important questions in life."[5]

He's right.

It's confusing when so many equally smart and educated people come to such radically different conclusions about this issue. I don't want to pretend like this is an easy question to answer. It's not. It's gut-wrenching, especially for those that have experienced the horrors of evil. However, my concern with the stories of people that have abandoned God because of the existence of evil is *not* the depth of their faith in God, but rather their commitment to a belief in evil!

I'm convinced that evil, far from disproving God's existence, is actually some of the best evidence *for* God. In fact, my own personal experience with evil has not weakened my belief in God, but strengthened it. This is the same conclusion that C.S. Lewis arrived at. He had originally adopted atheism because of the problem of evil, but he ultimately realized that it provided a far better argument *for* God. Speaking of evil, Lewis writes:

> My argument against God was that the universe seemed so cruel and unjust. But how had I got this idea of "just" and "unjust"? A man does not call a line crooked unless he has some idea of a straight line. What was I comparing this universe with when I called it unjust?[6]

My initial response whenever a person says to me, "I can't believe in God because there is too much evil in the world," is to simply ask, "Exactly, what do you mean by *evil?*" The response I usually get is a confused and uncertain one. They are convinced that evil exists, but as C.S. Lewis explained, most people are not exactly sure what evil is or why it shouldn't exist. It's wise then, before we continue, to define two significant terms that we often use without properly understanding them: evil and good.

Evil

Often, it's been said that evil is not a thing in itself, but rather that it's the absence of something. For example, darkness is just the absence of light. In the same way, evil is said to be the absence of good.

Now, this is a good start, but I think it's a little more than that: evil is also the *corruption* of good. After all, that's how we use and understand the word "evil." When people say that something is bad, wrong, or evil, what they mean to say is that the world ought not to be that way. We say that poverty and genocide are evil because they are a corruption of the way things should be—a world in which all people have enough food and are never murdered. Therefore, the idea of evil only makes sense if we already believe in good.

Take money for example. Counterfeit currency is the corruption of real currency. While you can have real currency without necessarily having counterfeit, it is impossible to have counterfeit currency unless real currency already exists. Similarly, evil could not exist if good did not first exist. Think about it. When we judge something as being evil, bad, or wrong, we are presupposing there is such a thing as good, right, and correct; we are acknowledging that there is a standard for the way things should be.

In the same way, when I say Raju and Reaksa experienced evil, I am really saying that what happened to them was wrong because there is a right. In essence, we are spotting the counterfeit of good and calling it evil.

But do we know what the real thing is? After all, when a bank teaches a teller how to spot counterfeit, they first teach them what real currency looks and feels like, because only then will they be able to spot the fake. So, if evil is the counterfeit, then good is the real thing—the standard by which we make moral judgments. But what *is* good and who decides?

Good

Christianity teaches that goodness is an attribute of God—a necessary expression of his character. This means that morality is not at God's whim. Something isn't good because God declared it to be so, as though he could change his mind, but rather because God *is* wholly good and he cannot change the essence of what he is.[7]

But what does it mean to say that God is good? How is goodness an attribute of God's nature? The Bible teaches that the one true God is a Trinity, one God who eternally exists as three distinct persons: Father, Son, and Holy Spirit. This piece of theology is significant because it means that God embodies relationship. More than that, God demonstrates the standard of right relationship within himself. His nature or essence is the standard.

Some people may object to rooting goodness in the nature of God and ask, "Why can't I, or society at large, be the standard of goodness?" The reason is that if people, or societies, were the standard of goodness, then that standard could change depending on the time or place. It would be subjective. Yet, we all acknowledge the existence of a moral law or standard which all people in all times are subject to. Is there ever a time when rape is morally good? If the standard of goodness is rooted in societies, you would have to say that there might be a time when that could be true. Yet, we all instinctively know that rape has never been, and never will be, morally good. There is a universal standard of goodness that is unalterable by people and must, therefore, be found outside of ourselves and rooted in God.

It's easy to make some false assumptions here. So, let's take a moment to clarify what I'm *not* saying. I am not saying that you need to believe in God in order to do good things. I'm also not saying that you can't develop or formulate an ethical life without referring to God. I believe you can. Atheists can do good things. What I *am* saying is that without God, good and evil wouldn't exist. We would have no concept of wrong, because there wouldn't be an objective or standard of right. I believe that all people are aware of moral and immoral behaviour because objective moral values do exist, whether we acknowledge their origin as being from God or not.

A good example of this took place after World War II in Nuremberg, Germany, when the Nazis were charged with crimes against humanity. Before the Nuremberg Trials could begin, there was a problem: how to prosecute the Nazis. They couldn't be tried by the laws of the Allied Forces because the crimes took place in Germany. Yet, they couldn't be prosecuted under German law because what they had done was not illegal in Germany. Hitler and his party had been very careful to pass laws in order to ensure that their heinous actions were sanctioned by German legislation. Therefore, in order to declare that the Nazi's actions were criminal, the judges had to appeal to a moral authority that was higher than a person or a society.[8] This was accomplished by using the Rule According to Higher Law, a law above man's law. Although this law was purposely kept unwritten and undefined, it clearly refers to a universal moral standard, outside of ourselves, which we all know exists. This is the same universal moral law that Martin Luther King Jr. referred to in his famous *Letter from a Birmingham Jail*:

> A just law is a man-made code that squares with the moral law or the law of God... An unjust law is a code that is out of harmony with the moral law. To put it in terms of Saint Thomas Aquinas: 'An unjust law is a human law not rooted in eternal law and natural law...'[9]

Interestingly, Adolf Hitler was well aware of God's law or standard (eternal law). He knew that the Holocaust was wrong. History tells us that he was careful not to sign anything or be too closely tied to the Holocaust. Rather, the orders were all given in secret and mostly verbally. In fact, Hitler was so successful at not leaving any traces, that some authors have incorrectly argued that Hitler didn't even know about the Holocaust.[10] I can't help but ask: if he was utterly convinced that his actions were morally right, then why wouldn't he want to be given credit for them? The only explanation is that he knew that killing people was wrong and he didn't want to be held responsible for the ghastly evils being committed.

We are all aware that some things are truly wrong, no matter what anyone or any society says. But is God really necessary for objective moral values to exist?

Some argue that morality is objective because a principle is the standard. For example, I once had a conversation with an atheist who argued for morality from percentages. She was convinced that humans are required to care for one another because of the large percentage of DNA that we share. It seemed reasonable, so I asked, "If we need to care for people because we share similar DNA, then what about a chimpanzee?" Her reply was quick and confident, "Yes." Then I asked, "Do I need to care for squirrels?" Her reply came a little slower, but was still a firm, "Yes." I then asked, "what about slugs?" The reply was even slower and more hesitant, but eventually she said, "Yes." I then asked, "What about plants? I mean, at exactly what percentage do I mow the lawn or not?" With that, she smiled. The point I was making was that her principle was ultimately subjective. She had become the arbiter of morality by determining the correct percentages. That's the problem with principles: who decides what they are?

To get around this, some people try to base morality on a general principle, rather than an individual one. The most common approach is to say that whatever contributes to human flourishing is good and whatever detracts from it is bad. Yet, here again is the same problem. Who says that human flourishing is good? What kind of flourishing is good? Even though human flourishing may seem to be a reasonable conclusion, being that it can be mutually beneficial, who says that I should behave reasonably? Why is being reasonable good and being unreasonable bad? As well, isn't a principle like that a little presumptuous? I mean what would stop a group of people from claiming that superior position? Who's to say that my flourishing isn't more important than your flourishing?

Notice what is continually happening here: morality is tied to personhood. Morality can't just exist on its own—it needs a lawgiver.[11] So, either people are the standard of morality or God is. Yet, we all know that morality is not solely determined by people. The Bible says that God's law is written on our hearts, meaning that we are all aware of an objective moral law above man's law that we are accountable to.[12] Perhaps this is why, upon seeing or experiencing evil, people naturally tend to hold God responsible and question his existence. Yet, as we have been discussing, without God there is no objective moral standard.

Honest Atheists

It is important to note that honest atheists agree with the conclusion that without God, there are no objective moral values. Richard Dawkins famously said, "The universe we observe has precisely the properties we should expect if there is, at bottom, no design, no purpose, no evil and no good, nothing but blind pitiless indifference."[13] Alex Rosenberg, a Philosophy professor from Duke University, wrote a manifesto on atheism in which he chides any atheist who clings to the concept of objective moral values. He says:

> What is the purpose of the universe? There is none.
> What is the meaning of life? Ditto.
> Is there free will? Not a chance.
> What is the difference between right and wrong, good

and bad? There is no moral difference between them.
Why should I be moral? Because it makes you feel better
than being immoral.

Is abortion, euthanasia, suicide, paying taxes, foreign aid,
or anything else you don't like forbidden, permissible,
or sometimes obligatory? Anything goes.[14]

The problem remains. None of those answers are true and we all
know it! Everyone has an innate awareness of morality, that some
things are objectively right and others are objectively wrong, and
that those things will not change over time or culture. The very
passion with which all people condemn the evil of this world
demonstrates our awareness of it.

This point was powerfully made during a debate between Alex
Rosenberg and William Lane Craig on the existence of God.
Midway through the debate, Rosenberg begins to explain his
personal disgust over evil:

> As we know, it's obvious that there is plenty of suffering
> in the world, both man made and natural suffering...I
> need to make something of my own personal history
> clear here. There are a lot of responses to the problem
> of evil that I find morally offensive, and I find them
> morally offensive for a certain reason. I'm the child of
> holocaust survivors. All of my family, except my parents,
> were killed by the Nazis including two half brothers of
> mine.[15]

Clearly emotionally pained by his family's experience with evil,
Rosenberg seems not only to believe that evil exists, but also to be
disgusted by it. As the debate continues, he makes a remarkable
admission. He challenges Craig saying:

In all honesty, if Dr. Craig could provide me with any kind of a logical, coherent account that could reconcile the evident fact of the horrors of human and infrahuman life on this planet over the last 3.5 billion years with the existence of a benevolent omnipotent agent, then I will turn Christian.

Wow!

His statements shocked me. After all, isn't it odd that someone who does not believe in the existence of evil is so troubled by it? If he doesn't think people have free will, then why is he so upset about the holocaust? Shouldn't he blame physics? It would seem that he *does* believe in a moral difference between good and evil after all, and that, in fact, "anything goes" is not correct. The issue for Alex Rosenberg is how to understand an all-powerful and loving God in the face of evil. Sadly, his conclusion is to reject God's existence.

However, here is the problem: taking God out of the equation doesn't make the problem of evil better—it makes it worse! Without God, we lose all grounds on which we can even talk about evil and good. Likewise, what justice is there in a world without God? Does this mean that people suffer in vain or that people who murder entire families have done no wrong? Will they never be held accountable?

Are you prepared to view what happened to Raju and Reaksa as blind, pitiless indifference?

In contrast, the existence of God allows us to do the very thing we so desperately desire—to condemn the evil of this world as wicked and deserving of judgment! author and Christian thinker, Os Guinness was right when he said:

Absolute evil calls for absolute judgment. Instinctively and intuitively, we cry out for the unconditional to condemn evil unconditionally. The atheist who lets fly "Goddammit!" in the face of evil is right, not wrong. It is a signal of transcendence, a pointer toward a better possibility—and unwittingly a prayer.[16]

I repeat that prayer every time I hear of yet another atrocity in our world. Not only is God essential for understanding the good, but also for us to condemn evil and ultimately, to find freedom and healing from it.

The Heart of the Question

Let's re-examine the statement: "I can't believe in God because there's too much evil in the world." Without a good God, there could be no such thing as evil. Yet, here we find ourselves desperate to condemn the very thing that doesn't exist. It's like saying, "I cannot believe in good because there's too much corruption of good in the world," or "I cannot believe in currency because there's too much counterfeit currency in the world." The statement is self-refuting; it seeks to disprove the very thing the person seems adamantly to believe—that there is a standard of goodness. What they don't recognize is that God is that standard that allows them to make sense of, and ultimately to condemn, the evil of this world.

Yet, if that's the case, if God has to exist for objective morality to exist, then who is responsible for evil?

God?

Rosenberg said that he was willing to throw his entire worldview out the window if only one question can be answered: Why does God allow evil?

In the Beginning

Any exploration into where evil came from and why God allows it has to start at the beginning—with how God created the world. The Bible begins with the book of Genesis, which tells us that God created a world that was wholly good. There was no moral corruption in it. However, there was the *potential* for corruption. This is because God created both angels and mankind with free will, which means the freedom to do what you want to do, whether that includes following God or not.

The Bible explains that Satan, an angel, was the first to corrupt God's goodness. We don't know all of the details of how and why Satan chose evil, but apparently he, and the angels that followed him, had a similar free will to that which humans have. The Genesis account, however, is focused on telling us *our* story: the story of how God made Adam and Eve, the first humans, to live in perfect relationship with God and each other in the Garden of Eden.[17] However, because they were made free, Adam and Eve contained the potential to break this relationship with God. This was made clear by God's command not to eat the fruit from the tree of the knowledge of good and evil.

One day, a serpent began to question God and twist his words, convincing Adam and Eve that God was holding out on them; he succeeded in causing them to question God and doubt his goodness. They chose to disobey God and eat the fruit. Adam and Eve's free will contained within it the potential for evil and, as they opened their minds and closed their teeth on the forbidden fruit, the world changed through an act of rebellion. There was nothing magical about the fruit that brought evil into the world; rather, it was the wrong act in a right world that created evil.

As a consequence for their actions, Adam and Eve received the "sight" promised by the serpent, but it was not as they expected. Where once they had good and beautiful garments of naked innocence, now they had only pitiful coverings of shame and disgrace. Their original purity had been stained and corrupted. Their relationships with God and with each other were now broken and they found themselves hiding from God. Essentially, when they went seeking their own "good," they instead created counterfeit good, corrupting themselves and all of creation.

Thus, the Bible makes it very clear that God did not create evil.

Angels and people did that.

Yet, if God is both all-powerful and all-good, why would he allow them to choose something so terrible?

Love's Problem

There have been many suggested answers to this question. The most helpful is the free will defense. It's called a defense because its purpose is not to *answer* the question. The truth of the matter is that we don't know why God allowed, and continues to allow, evil. It is a mystery. The prophet Isaiah said that God's ways and thoughts are higher than ours, and he hasn't seen fit to explain everything to us.[18] We have our ideas, but in the end, it is a question that will require an audience with God.

Therefore, the free will defense merely demonstrates that the existence of evil is not a dilemma. Whether or not you believe this is the correct answer is not the point. It merely shows that we are not dealing with a logical contradiction.

The classic dilemma or contradiction says that in the face of evil, one must accept that either God is not all-good or he is not all-powerful, both of which would stand in contradiction to the Christian understanding of the nature of God. However, what if there is a third option?

Could God have a good reason for allowing evil?

I believe that he does. To understand this, think about how God could have created the world. First, he could have chosen not to create the world at all. Then there would be no evil, but there also would not be anything. It's not a very good option.

Second, God could have created a world with creatures that have no free will. In this case, there would be no morality whatsoever. It would be a world full of robot-people, who only do what God programs them to do. Sure, they would have no vices, but they would also have no virtues. It stands to reason: would this type of world be even worth creating? It certainly wouldn't be if your aim is relationship, since true relationship is impossible with a mere robot.

Third, some suggest that God could have created a world with free creatures, but then he could just intervene all the time to stop them from choosing wrongly. I have to admit that I struggle to even understand how this type of world could be possible. I mean, how often should God intervene? All of the time, so no evil occurs? Some of the time, so only the really bad evil doesn't occur? Where's the line to know the difference? The problem with this view is the same problem as the world with no free will whatsoever: in a world without consequences, our actions don't mean anything at all and therefore we don't really have free will. As Christian thinker Clay Jones writes:

If God intervened "all the time," then our actions wouldn't mean anything. In fact, it would be a cartoon world. Johnny could be cutting his steak with a knife and the next moment jab it into his little brother, but the knife would turn to rubber and everyone at the table could laugh heartily...If our actions are to mean anything at all, then natural laws must work in regular ways...Of course, God could have made the world such that every time we looked up we saw a flaming sword dangling over our heads with the knowledge that the slightest rebellion would result in our immediate dismemberment. Then everyone would at least feign being a God-follower, wouldn't they? But feigned loyalty is no more than rebellion waiting for an opportunity.[19]

The third option is therefore very much like the second. If God constantly stopped us from choosing wrongly, then we wouldn't have true free will.

The fourth and only real option is that God created a world with free creatures that have the possibility to choose both good and evil. If God is both all-good and all-powerful, then it would follow that this is his best option, since it is the only world with real choices. We all know that morality requires free will; in order to choose good, there needs to be the option to not choose good. Perhaps then, this is why God allows evil: in order to allow the most noble of all ethics, the ability to choose love. This is the conclusion that C.S. Lewis came to. He writes:

Free will, though it makes evil possible, is also the only thing that makes possible any love or goodness or joy worth having...The happiness which God designs for His higher creatures is the happiness of being freely,

> voluntarily united to Him and to each other in an ecstasy
> of love and delights...And for that they must be free.[20]

This means that it's logically possible to have free will without evil; yet, the very nature of freedom means that God could not guarantee that. For God, it was worth the risk. Actually, God knew that we *would* corrupt his goodness, yet he created us anyway. This is troubling for many people. I mean, why create people if you know that they are going to do evil? Yet, isn't this the same challenge that every parent faces? Why have children when you *know* that they are going to disobey you?

God created us anyway because he loves us. The Bible says, "while we were still sinners, Christ died for us."[21] By demonstrating the depths of his love for us, we see and experience the glory of God. He is good. This fallen world, then, is the best way to a better world, a world with love. The cost of experiencing the beauty and depths of love is the real possibility of its vile opposite.

The Problem of Evil

Far from evil disproving the existence of God, morality actually demands the existence of God and is compatible with a loving, powerful Creator who allows evil for an unknown purpose, perhaps in order to ensure humankind's free will so that we can live in true relationship with God and people. That's all well and good, but for a lot of people, these explanations just don't go far enough.

I mean, what about hell?

Now, the word "hell" is not found in the Bible, but the concept of hell is. The Bible teaches that any sin, any wrongdoing whatsoever, will one day be judged by God. Jesus used powerful imagery to describe how awful this coming judgment will be. He said:

As the weeds are pulled up and burned in the fire, so it will be at the end of the age. The Son of Man will send out his angels, and they will weed out of his kingdom everything that causes sin and all who do evil. They will throw them into the blazing furnace, where there will be weeping and gnashing of teeth.[22]

Needless to say, these images have fueled the imaginations of people across the centuries. Although people throughout history have speculated about the exact nature of God's judgment, the reality is that we don't know what the punishment of hell will be like. Theologian William Crockett says, "The words of Jesus and the Apostles tell us that the final abode of the wicked will be a place of awful reckoning, but specifically what that reckoning will be, we cannot know for certain until we pass beyond this life."[23]

What we do know about hell is that it exists, it's awful, and you don't want to go there. Jesus uses some strong words and images to describe an unimaginably awful reality that he does not want you to experience. That's the point of Jesus' teaching about God's coming judgment: he's warning you. God does not want you to experience his final judgment of evil.

I Am a Murdering Adulterer

But hold on a second. If God doesn't want us to go to hell, then why is there hell in the first place? I mean, how does the existence of hell square with the existence of an all-loving, all-powerful God?

Most people who ask this type of question, haven't really thought through the consequences of evil, or what it means to say that people are sinful and that God is holy. The Bible is very clear that all people are sinful and thus are spiritually dead and severed from relationship with God. Romans 3:23 says that "all have sinned and fall short of the glory of God." Have you ever seriously thought about that? I mean, it says *all* people.

Most people have trouble with this concept because most people see themselves as good people who don't deserve judgment. That's all fine for the murderers and rapists, most of us think, but what about all the good people? I mean, most people are relatively good, aren't they?

Actually, Jesus went out of his way to show that there is no such thing as a good person. Perhaps the most poignant example is found in Matthew 5. Jesus was travelling through an area called Galilee, teaching the people wherever he went. A large crowd gathered and so Jesus climbed up a hill, stood there, and preached what is often called the Sermon on the Mount. It's a convicting sermon where Jesus continually takes people's assumptions and knocks them to the ground. In the middle of it, Jesus said, "You have heard that it was said to the people long ago, 'Do not murder, and anyone who murders will be subject to judgment.' But I tell you that anyone who is angry with his brother will be subject to judgment."[24]

Now that's a convicting statement! After all, when we think about morality, we all think about which actions are right and which actions are wrong. Everybody knows that actually murdering someone is wrong. However, Jesus turned this view of morality upside down and said that it's so much deeper than that. Morality is about more than just *doing* right and wrong actions, it's about having right and wrong *desires*. Desires are something that we can hide from the world; we can fool everyone and even ourselves into thinking that we are a good person, but Jesus says that we will really be judged by the condition of our heart, and that makes us all guilty murderers. I mean, what haven't you desired in your anger? By that standard, I murder people all the time.

Yet just in case anyone is confused about Jesus' point, he immediately repeats it in a different way. He says, "You have heard that it was said, 'You shall not commit adultery.' But I tell you that anyone who looks at a woman lustfully has already committed adultery with her in his heart."[25] You see, goodness is not about what you do, it's about who you are. We may be able to exert some self-control when it comes to our actions, but the instincts of our heart reveal us for the evil murdering adulterers that we really are. This is why the Apostle Paul can write in the book of Romans, "There is no one righteous, not even one; there is no one who understands; there is no one who seeks God."[26] This passage reminds us that the fundamental problem of humanity is not ignorance, but rebellion. The Bible consistently reminds us that each of us are born with a nature of counterfeit-good, a bent toward breaking relationship with God and each other.

We are responsible for the evil we do, not God.

I Am Not Good

This has been a difficult lesson for us to learn. Instead of admitting our sinfulness, we want to blame anyone or anything else. In *The Republic*, Plato tries to convince his audience that humanity's primary issue is ignorance. He is well aware of people's weaknesses when it comes to power and corruption, but he remains confident that, with a proper education, it is possible for humanity to wield power appropriately. Yet, here we are, over two thousand years later, and despite having the highest levels of information and education in history, the world is still full of political corruption and moral degradation. History has consistently taught that Plato was wrong: our corruption is much deeper than any education can fix.

If we ever doubt that the human heart is naturally wicked, we only need to look at the twentieth century, the bloodiest century in the history of the world, to see example after example. We may be tempted to look at people like Hitler, Stalin, or Mao, and write them off as psychopaths—unfortunate exceptions in an otherwise decent species. However, digging deeper reveals that evil is not unusual—it's incredibly *ordinary*.

The ordinariness of evil is described well by Langdon Gilkey, an American who was interned in a Japanese camp in China during World War II. Unlike other work camps, here the Japanese only guarded the walls and provided supplies, while the rest of the day-to-day organization and operations were left to the prisoners themselves. Gilkey, educated in philosophy at Harvard, decided to view the situation as a grand experiment. After all, the camp was filled with some of the best of the west: doctors, lawyers, missionaries, and business people from Great Britain, America, and Australia. Like most secularists, Gilkey believed that people were essentially moral creatures. So, if this were an opportunity to see humanity at its most raw and honest, what would happen in the camp when push came to shove?

Although the situation in the camp started out optimistically, it quickly plunged into chaos. Nobody chose the moral high ground in the way that a belief in essential human goodness would predict. Instead, people consistently looked out only for the interests of themselves and their families. They stole food and supplies whenever possible. They cruelly refused to share with those in need. They avoided volunteer work. They declined to uphold justice and, above all, they rationalized their evil behaviour. In his book, *Shantung Compound*, he writes:

> My ideas as to what people were like and as to what motivated their actions were undergoing a radical revision. People generally seemed to be much less rational and much more selfish than I had ever guessed, not at all the "nice folk" I had always thought them to be. They did not decide to do things because it would be reasonable and moral to act in that way; but because that course of action suited their self-interest... Strangely enough, I still kept expecting the opposite... Nothing indicates so clearly the fixed belief in the innate goodness of humans as does this confidence that when the chips are down, and we are revealed for what we "really are," we will be good to each other. Nothing could be so totally in error.[27]

To summarize what he discovered about the human condition, Gilkey quotes Bertolt Brecht's play *The Threepenny Opera*, saying, "Even saintly folk will act like sinners unless they get their customary dinners."

Now remember, these people weren't psychopaths. They were just average people, like you and me. We may think that we would never behave like that, that we are good people at our core. Yet, history continually shows us that when put into difficult situations, most people will act far worse than they care to admit.[28] When push comes to shove, our inherent goodness turns out to be just a delusion of grandeur.[29]

We don't need to look to such extremes to see the obvious. The anonymity of the Internet has given us a window into the human heart like never before. A quick scan of the comments section of a YouTube video, blog post, or news article will quickly purge one of any doubts concerning human depravity.

Holy, Holy, Holy

Once we start to really understand the depths of human evilness, of *our own* evilness, it starts to change our perspective on hell. But in order to complete our perspective, we need to understand one more thing, the opposite of human sinfulness: God's holiness.

God's holiness is a pivotal point for understanding hell because, without it, hell often seems like a huge over-reaction. I mean, so we sin sometimes—what's the big deal?

Denny Burk, a theologian and author, explains hell and God's holiness with a graphic illustration. He says:

> If you were to discover a little boy pulling the legs off of a grasshopper, you would think it strange and perhaps a little bizarre. If the same little boy were pulling the legs off of a frog, that would be a bit more disturbing. If it were a bird, you would probably scold him and inform his parents. If it were a puppy, that would be too

shocking to tolerate. You would intervene. If it were a little baby, it would be so reprehensible and tragic that you would risk your own life to protect the baby. What's the difference in each of these scenarios? The sin is the same (pulling the limbs off). The only difference is the one sinned against (from a grasshopper to a baby). The more noble and valuable the creature, the more heinous and reprehensible the sin.

And so it is with God. If God were a grasshopper, then to sin against Him wouldn't be such a big deal and [hell] wouldn't be necessary. But God isn't a grasshopper, He's the most precious, valuable, beautiful being in the universe...Our sin seems small because we regard God as small. And thus the penalty of hell...always seems like an overreaction on God's part. If we knew God better, we wouldn't think like that.[30]

You see, evil is more than just the bad things we do—it's about not having relationship. The main consequence of evil is that of separation. Evil separates people from the purpose they were created for, it separates people from each other, and primarily, it separates us from relationship with God. This is why Mother Teresa described poverty not as an absence of material things, but as an absence of love. She recognized that the very worst thing in the world, even worse than being without food, is being without relationship.[31]

Keep in mind that God, because of his perfection, cannot be in relationship with evil. Satan was removed from heaven and Adam and Eve were expelled from the Garden of Eden not because they were a threat to God, but because God was a threat to them. It's not like God was fleeing from evil lest he be corrupted—God is incorruptible! Rather, removing them from his presence was an act of mercy. He was sparing them; for if they, the corrupted, were to stand in the presence of God in all his glory, they would be destroyed.

That's what hell is all about. It's not an over-reaction—it's justice.

Stuck in Hell

This is the part about hell that we need to get right. A lot of people misunderstand hell to be some kind of theological exam: pass and you make it to heaven; fail and you're going to hell. For this reason, I think a lot of people imagine hell as a place full of people that don't want to be there. They imagine that God is some kind of eternal kill-joy who forces people to stay in hell to punish their ignorance or misfortune; they wish they had passed the test, but God was just too harsh.

This view of hell reminds me of when my wife gave birth to our first child. Although I have it on good authority from my wife that giving birth *is* hell, that's not what I'm getting at! Instead, I'm referring to the fact that I almost missed welcoming my first child into the world!

I can still remember waking up that day in Guatemala, where I was leading a mission trip. It was our second-to-last day and I opened my email to find a message from a friend who told me that my wife had unexpectedly gone into labor early. My heart fell out of my chest and hit the floor. I was a wreck as the implications hit me. I wasn't there to support my wife through the delivery and I was going to miss the birth of our first child. It was a feeling that is impossible to put into words.

I didn't pack a thing.

I just walked straight to the missionary and said, "You have to take me to the airport!" At the airport, I searched frantically for a flight that was heading anywhere near Vancouver, BC. No luck. Literally, the closest flights I could find were headed to either Mexico City or Miami. Heartbroken, I finally collapsed onto the middle of the airport floor. Yeah, I was being a bit of a drama queen, but I was truly a mess. More than anything, I wanted out of that airport!

Eventually, after a major pity party, I picked myself up off the floor to go check one more airline. Amazingly, they had a flight to Vancouver that left in only two hours. After an agonizing day, I finally made it to the hospital, and thirty minutes later, my wife went into full labour and I welcomed our son into the world.

I tell that story because I think many people think that's what hell is like: being stuck in a place you desperately want to get out of. So, we shake our fist at God and say, "How could you? How can you send so many people to hell?"

However, it is our view of hell that is flawed. Hell is not full of people who don't want to be there. Sadly, the Bible teaches that hell is full of people who willingly chose to be there. Charles Spurgeon says it this way: "It is the will of God that saves—it is the will of man that damns."[32] In his book *The Great Divorce*, C.S. Lewis says a similar thing, "There are only two kinds of people in the end: those who say to God, 'Thy will be done,' and those to whom God says, in the end, 'Thy will be done.'"[33] I think the concerns we have about hell are much deeper than God not giving people what they want.

Can I Trust You?

It's difficult for us to trust God. We are often filled with doubts and concerns...you know the ones; they fill our hypothetical questions. What about those people who live on a deserted island and have never had an opportunity to know God? Or what about the sincere Muslim or Buddhist—what will God do with them? This is often the complaint we raise against God. At least, I know I do.

But, then I must challenge myself: why do I automatically assume that God is unjust?

Perhaps the answer to these difficult questions is found in a much more basic question, like the one Adam and Eve faced in the garden: do I trust God? Do I trust that he is good and will do what is right? Often, when we raise hypothetical questions, what we are really doing is questioning God. We seem to think that God won't do what's good, but that we would.

The Bible warns us to take caution, for the heart of man is deceptively corrupt.[34] Do we honestly believe that we can judge better than God? If anything, this presumptuous attitude demonstrates the condition of our brokenness. The Bible makes it clear that God sees the heart and that he loves all people and wants to have relationship with them.[35] Likewise, Jesus tells us that those who seek will find, and that to those who knock, the door is opened.[36] The problem is that the Bible is also clear that this world is full of people in rebellion against God; they are not seeking or knocking. We must leave it to God to be able to judge the difference.

This is the conclusion that Mother Teresa came to as well. She wrestled deeply with the problem of evil, and at times it made her feel isolated from God. Yet, through the struggle, she decided to trust her savior. She trusted that he had a plan that was bigger than she could see from her perspective.

A God Who Suffers

In the face of evil, Mother Teresa ultimately turned to the cross of Christ, because that's where we are meant to turn. You see, ultimately, the existence of evil begs us for a solution. Can we ever be free of evil? Because of the cross of Jesus, we can say "yes."

In the Garden of Eden, Adam and Eve's sin brought evil into the world, forcing God out of relationship with his beloved creation. But, that's the amazing thing about the God that Christianity proclaims: he didn't leave us in that state. He could have—but he didn't. Instead, God made a promise to rescue us and restore everything back to its original purity and beauty. Way back at the fall of Adam and Eve, God promised to defeat evil.[37]

And he did.

At the cross.

All of the philosophical arguments about the problem of evil— the explanations about free will and the necessity of God's judgment—all of those are important. But, when we are right in the middle of suffering ourselves, when we see the evil in this world and recoil with horror, what we really need is to look at the cross of Jesus.

Christianity doesn't tell us of a God who is indifferent to our pain, or worse, is a maniacal monster who takes pleasure in it.

Instead, the Bible teaches that God so loved us that he was willing to send his Son down from the throne of heaven to enter into our pain. Jesus Christ, God's Son, lived a perfect life. He didn't deserve to suffer or die. Yet, he was beaten, he was mocked, he was abused, and he was brutally murdered—all for us. We deserve death, but he didn't.

That December when I served in Calcutta, the nativity story took on a much deeper significance for me. As I celebrated Christmas with the impoverished and the destitute, I realized that God had kept his promise. God entered into our suffering, as a baby. It was both an act of compassion and of war. He was willingly born into poverty with the mission to defeat evil; through his sacrifice on the cross, he did just that.

Looking to the cross of Christ is the thing that brought healing to Reaksa Himm. For years he raged against God, angry that he had lost his entire family. Then, Reaksa read the gospel of John. He writes:

> Where was God in my suffering? He was beside me, suffering with me, crying with me. Jesus became a man so that he could know the depths of human suffering, abandonment, loneliness and physical pain, right up to death and beyond. Only those who have known deep pain themselves can come alongside those who suffer: now I realised that God himself understands the pain. In fact he knows the path of pain intimately, because he once walked through it—for us.[38]

Eventually, Reaksa cried out to God:

> Lord God, I have tasted enough bitterness in my life.
> The picture of the killers are in my mind every day, and
> I have no peace but only hatred, anger and bitterness
> in my heart and soul. The fire of my anger burns in
> my heart, and it's destroying me. I can only make the
> decision to forgive. Father God, I ask you to grant me
> power to put out the fire that has been there for years.
> Grant me peace and clean my heart as I forgive those
> who killed my family.[39]

God answered that prayer. Eventually, Reaksa was even able
to return to Cambodia and find the men who murdered his
family, so that he could forgive them in person. If the existence
of evil is powerful evidence for the existence of God, how much
more is the ability to love in the face of evil? This is what God
demonstrated to us in Jesus: the world's greatest love in the face
of the world's greatest evil.

Conclusion

So, if God cares about evil enough that he sent his Son to
conquer it on the cross, then why do we still have to suffer now?

It's all about what comes after this life. Christianity teaches that
in this world we will have trouble, but that we are to take heart
because God has overcome the evils of this world and one day
we will live with him forever in heaven.[40] Just as we don't fully
understand the suffering of hell, we don't know fully the joys of
heaven. But God has promised us that even the greatest thing
on earth is but a mere hint of what is yet to come. Perhaps the
evils of this world are our preparation for that glorious day. Life
is a long and necessary lesson of the knowledge of good and evil,

perhaps in order to ensure that when we finally are united with God, we will never be tempted to rebel again.

The Apostle Paul understood that his temporal sufferings were nothing in comparison to an eternity spent with the God who loved him.[41] I think that you will agree that people will endure all kinds of hardship in light of a greater good. How much more should people set their sights on the glory of heaven to come! Heaven is not some kind of bribe to get us to love God, instead it is love perfected. It is the one place where things are the way they should be—wholly good. I believe that the evil we experience on this temporal earth, even the truly horrid evils, such as the suffering that Raju and Reaksa went through, become insignificant in the light of an eternity in heaven with God. Saying that does not diminish their pain and suffering; rather it asserts that the true joy of heaven is beyond anything we can even think or imagine.

Yet many Christians live as though heaven is merely a p.s. to their life story. This was not what Jesus taught; nor was it how his disciples lived. Heaven was everything they lived, suffered, and hoped for. The Apostle Paul did not endure shipwrecks, beatings, and imprisonment with his sights on earth, but with his eyes lifted to heaven. In a letter to the church in Corinth, he wrote, "For our light and momentary troubles are achieving for us an eternal glory that far outweighs them all. So we fix our eyes not on what is seen, but on what is unseen, since what is seen is temporary, but what is unseen is eternal."[42]

But is there such a thing as eternity? It seems that everything we have talked about, from the meaning of life to the problem of evil, depends on it. That's why our final question is, "Is there life after death?"

Chapter Five

Is There Life After Death?

When our plane touched down in Luxor, Egypt, it felt like we had travelled back in time. My wife and I had both recently completed degrees in Biblical Studies. After so many years digesting textbooks, we were excited to finally be exploring the Biblical lands for ourselves. For two months during our world tour, we backpacked up Egypt, through the Sinai Peninsula, and into Israel, before finishing our trip in Jordan. We saw countless historic sites and toured through some amazing places. Yet, despite all of the significant things we saw, what truly made the pages of history come alive was the time we spent with a young man named Wesley.

We met Wesley in Israel, through a series of unusual events. We had just arrived in Galilee and were excited to start exploring the Biblical sites; however, our Indiana Jones-style dreams were abruptly cut short. Unbeknownst to us, we had arrived just in time for a national holiday and all transportation was shut down. We were stuck. After much searching and pleading, we realized that our only options were to walk or rent some bikes. The distance we had to travel, combined with the oppressive heat, meant that neither was a viable option.

Not wanting to waste the day, we went for a walk along the Sea of Galilee, which is more commonly known today as Lake Kinneret. It wasn't long into our walk when we came upon a fishing boat for hire that was a replica from the time of Christ. With a mixture of excitement and desperation, I asked the captain if we could rent the boat. It was impossible to hide our disappointment as he informed us that it had actually been booked months in advance. Yet, to our surprise, he offered to ask if the party chartering it would let us come aboard and join them. I didn't want to intrude, but we literally had nothing else going; it was worth a try. A few minutes later, the captain came back with a South African man who greeted us warmly, saying, "You're welcome to come aboard with us, but it might get a little weird." He then paused and added, "It might get a little crazy." This caught me by surprise and I hesitantly replied "Okay..." But soon my curiosity got the best of me—I wanted to see weird and crazy! So, we accepted the offer with a firm handshake and climbed aboard.

Upon boarding the small wooden sailboat, we were greeted by a lovely South African family—even Grandma was there. As we set sail for the center of the lake that morning, it felt like we were fading into Biblical times as all signs of civilization disappeared into the fog hovering over the quiet waters. Sitting as far away from the family as we could manage, we tried to enjoy the peaceful experience. Yet, at the same time, we were nervously waiting for the weird and crazy to begin. When we reached the middle of the lake, the captain dropped the sails, and that's when things got interesting. The family circled together, pulled out a guitar, and began to pray and sing to God. To our delight, it turned out that they were one of those crazy Christian families! My wife and I instantly recognized the song and asked to join in their amazing worship service on the lake.

Later on, the family told us that there was a large van waiting for them on the other side of the lake. Turns out that the van had two extra seats, and so they invited us to join them for a day of sightseeing! It was a twenty-first century Bible story in the making! Excitedly, we accepted their invitation, not fully knowing how special their offer really was.

It wasn't until the last site of the day that my wife and I learned the significance of their vacation together. After a wonderful day of seeing history come alive, the family had saved the most significant for last; this was the location they anticipated seeing more than any other. As the van pulled up along the shore of the lake, I was surprised by how unassuming the location was. I didn't notice any signs or any other tourists. As we all piled out of the van, 22-year-old Wesley, the youngest son in the family, went around to the back with his brother-in-law and began unloading a wheelchair. This was the first time they had brought the wheelchair out, and to my surprise, Wesley sat in it. I thought Wesley was joking around and was just about to tell him to get out of Grandma's chair; but then I realized that this was not a joke.

Wesley's mom was standing beside me, with her hands covering her face. She was sobbing uncontrollably while her family came alongside her, gently putting their arms around her. No one spoke; it was obvious that they all knew her pain. It was only my wife and I who were confused. Nothing had previously tipped us off that something unusual was up. As they wheeled Wesley down to the lake, one of the brothers came beside us and said, "You're probably wondering what's going on." My wife and I met eyes with him and nodded. "Wesley is dying," he said. He went on to explain that Wesley had recently been diagnosed with cancer and been given only three months to live. We had no idea. He was young and looked healthy. It was humbling to realize that this was the family's last vacation together and here they had invited us to share the day with them!

Everyone continued walking down to the water's edge, but Wesley's mom didn't stop. She just walked right into the lake, all the way up to her waist, and remained there weeping. Wesley was wheeled to the shore, where he quietly gazed across the lake. Then, Wesley's father walked over to an outcropping on the shore, opened his Bible, and began to read aloud. Everyone quietly listened as he read from the Gospel of John. While he read, I looked around and noticed a metal plate on a rock with the words "This is Holy Ground." I began to wonder: where are we? And why is this place so special to this family?

As Wesley's father continued to read, I recognized the story from John 21 which revealed the significance of our location. This unassuming place on the shore of the lake was one of the places where Jesus met with his disciples after returning from the dead.

The disciples had spent the night fishing with no success when suddenly a man walked up along the shore and called out to the men in the boat. He asked them how the fishing was going and, after learning of their dry spell, he encouraged the men to cast their net on the other side of the boat. Now, this suggestion must have made them suspicious. After all, the Gospel of Luke reports that a similar situation had happened years earlier, when Jesus had first called his disciples.[1] Just like last time, when they pulled their nets up from the other side of the boat, they were full of fish. Now, they knew without a doubt that it was the risen Jesus on the shore. Peter was so excited to see Jesus that he couldn't wait another second; even though the boat was only a short distance from shore, Peter threw himself into the water and swam toward Jesus.

Then, using some of the fish that they had just caught, Jesus cooked up breakfast for the disciples, right there on the beach. Afterward, the risen Messiah asked Peter three life-changing questions: Do you love me? Do you love me? Do you love me? Three times, Peter answered, "Yes," leading Jesus to reinstate Peter as a disciple. The significance of why Jesus asked him the same question three times was not lost on Peter. Before Jesus had been crucified, Peter had zealously vowed to die for Jesus. Yet, after Jesus was arrested, Peter not only abandoned Jesus, but three times he denied having anything to do with this "King of the Jews." After disowning Jesus, Peter watched as his friend, teacher, and Messiah died a shameful public execution by Roman crucifixion. Peter was devastated. Now, here on these shores, where Peter was first called to be a disciple, he was being called again.

As Wesley's father continued to read, I began to realize why this site was so important to the family. This was the spot where Peter, nearly the same age as Wesley, received his own death sentence. Jesus told Peter that the cost of following him had not changed; it would still cost Peter everything. In fact, Jesus informed Peter that he would certainly be killed if he continued to follow after him. Peter, true to character, asked Jesus a question that most people would ask given such circumstances. Pointing his finger at John, a fellow disciple and friend, Peter asked, "Jesus, what about him?" In other words, "tell me he is going to suffer and die at least as bad as me!" At this, Jesus looked at Peter and said, "If I want him to remain alive until I return, what is that to you? *You* must follow me."[2]

Jesus was getting at the heart of the issue—will you trust me, Peter? The reality is that death is waiting for us all, some sooner than others. We can't control the trials that will come our way, but we can control whom we will serve and trust in the midst of those challenges. Peter made his choice that day, a choice that, as history reports, cost him his life.

As Wesley's father closed his Bible and began to pray, I reflected on what had happened two thousand years ago on these very shores, that inspired people like Peter and now Wesley, to face death with such courage.

Death is a reality we will all face. Some have more or less time than others, but we're all terminal. It doesn't matter your age or your relative health. The truth is that the only thing stopping you from witnessing everyone you love and care for die, is your own death. It's not surprising then, that one of the fundamental concerns of humanity is this: Is there life after death?

But have you ever considered what is meant by that question?

I don't know anyone that truly desires to live forever. What Wesley's family made clear to me that day is that the real question we are asking is: "Is there relationship after death?" The real fear in dying is the relational separation that it brings. That's why death is so hard on the living.

A Death Experience

Death is a question that has haunted humanity from the very beginning. It is the inescapable unknown into which everyone must venture. Does death lead to an eternal nothing or an eternal something? Is it possible to know what lies beyond the grave, if anything?

Our culture is fascinated by near death experiences.[3] We hope that people who've briefly peered over the edge can give us a small glimpse into the unknown. Yet, though we find the clues in these stories fascinating, what we need is not the testimony of a *near* death experience, but that of a *death* experience. If we want conclusive evidence that there is life after death, it would require the witness of a person that has *fully* experienced death.

The problem is: people don't return from the grave.

At least, not usually. History does however record one convincing account of a person that had a death experience—Jesus Christ. In fact, the entire Christian faith is based on that single idea: that Jesus lived, died, and lives again. This is significant because Jesus claimed to be the author of life and to offer eternal relational life with God. By overcoming death, he proved it.

To put it clearly: if Jesus rose from the dead, then we, like Wesley and his family, have hope that Jesus is who he claimed to be and that there is life after death. If Jesus stayed in the grave, then Jesus was not who he claimed to be, the entire Christian faith is futile, and we know nothing about what happens after death.[4]

Obviously, the question of whether Jesus rose from the dead is of the utmost importance. Everything leads up to this question and hinges on it. Either Jesus rose from the dead or he did not. But can we know if it's true? What information do we have about what happened in Jerusalem two thousand years ago?

Did Jesus Even Exist?

Some people have argued that we have virtually no information about what happened at the time of Christ. In fact, some have even argued that Jesus didn't exist as a historical person—they argue that he is a myth that was made up many years later. There have been a number of popular books that have taken this idea of the "Jesus myth" into all sorts of creative directions.

However, what might surprise you is that all serious historians know that Jesus existed as a real person. Even skeptics of Christianity, such as Bart Ehrman, believe that Jesus was a historical person and that there is reliable information about him that is readily available. In his book *Did Jesus Exist?*, Ehrman writes:

> There are several points on which virtually all scholars of antiquity agree. Jesus was a Jewish man, known to be a preacher and teacher, who was crucified (a Roman form of execution) in Jerusalem during the reign of the Roman emperor Tiberius, when Pontius Pilate was the governor of Judea. Even though this is the view of nearly every trained scholar on the planet, it is not the view of a group of writers who are usually labeled, and often label themselves, mythicists.[5]

The idea that Jesus did not exist, or that his story is borrowed from pagan myths, is discredited by both Christian and non-Christian scholars. Virtually everyone is in agreement. But where did we get all of this information about Jesus? Just from the Bible? Can the Bible even be trusted as a source of information?

Ancient Writings

The New Testament is not the only source of information we have about Jesus. References to Jesus and his disciples also appear in the writings of the Jewish historian Josephus, the Roman historians Tacitus and Suetonius, and Roman magistrate and author Pliny the Younger. One of the most helpful passages for establishing data about Jesus is one called the *Testimonium Flavianum* from Josephus' work *Antiquities of the Jews*, written in 93-94 AD.

Most scholars doubt the complete authenticity of the *Testimonium Flavianum*, claiming that as Christian scribes made copies of the work they added to it over time in order to make Josephus more directly assert the claims of Christianity. However, most scholars also agree that even if the statement *was* expanded over time, its central premise remains the same; there is no doubt that Josephus did mention certain facts about Jesus. Many scholars, Bart Ehrman among them, advocate removing the contentious phrases from the passage in order to recapture what was probably Josephus' original statement, before the Christians embellished it.[6] In its conservative, pared-down form, the *Testimonium Flavianum* says:

> At that time there was a wise man called Jesus, and his conduct was good, and he was known to be virtuous. Many people among the Jews and the other nations became his disciples. Pilate condemned him to be crucified and to die. But those who had become his disciples did not abandon his discipleship. They reported that he had appeared to them three days after his crucifixion and that he was alive. Accordingly, he was perhaps the Messiah, concerning whom the prophets have reported wonders. And the tribe of the Christians, so named after him, has not disappeared to this day.[7]

146 | **THINKING?**

Because of this passage, there is a consensus among scholars that
Josephus did assert the existence of Jesus and at the very least,
make reference to his virtuous life, his reputation for miracles,
his death by crucifixion, and the spread of his followers.

However, it's important to appreciate that these extra-Biblical
sources for Jesus pale in comparison to the documents that make
up the New Testament. Yet, many people ask or wonder if the
documents that make up the New Testament are trustworthy.
Historians judge the trustworthiness of ancient sources based on
a few factors, for example: the number of ancient manuscripts
we have, how consistent they are with one another, and how
close our earliest copy is to when the work was originally written.
For example, of Greek historian Herodotus' masterpiece *The
Histories*, we only have 109 copies from antiquity and the earliest
manuscripts we have date from around 1,350 years after it was
originally written.[8] Likewise, Julius Caesar's *The Gallic Wars*
has about 251 preserved copies, with the earliest manuscript
coming from about 950 years after it was written. By far the best-
preserved classical work is Homer's *Iliad*, of which we have 1,757
manuscripts, with the earliest manuscript dating to around 400
years after it was written.

In stark contrast, for the New Testament, we have over 5,700
ancient manuscripts and fragments, the earliest of which date
to between 40-100 years after they were written. If you add in
manuscript copies written in other languages, such as Latin,
Armenian, Coptic, Slavic, and Ethiopian, the number of
manuscripts jumps by another 15,000. The incredible number
of manuscripts and fragments is a powerful demonstration of
Biblical accuracy and early authorship. Christian thinker Clay
Jones has done an extensive study on this bibliographic test for
the reliability of the New Testament. He says:

When one adds the fifteen thousand manuscripts in other languages, and then considers that almost the entire NT could be reproduced by the quotations of the early church fathers, one must maintain that... the NT remains in a class by itself: it is by far the most attested ancient work. This troubles skeptics because if they reject the transmissional reliability of the NT, then they must also consider unreliable all other manuscripts of antiquity. As John Warwick Montgomery has often related: "Some years ago, when I debated philosophy professor Avrum Stroll of the University of British Columbia on this point, he responded: 'All right. I'll throw out my knowledge of the classical world.' At which the chairman of the classics department cried: 'Good Lord, Avrum, not that!'[9]

The sheer number of manuscripts, as well as the consistency of them, shows us that the text of the New Testament has not been corrupted over time and we can reasonably believe that we are reading what the authors originally wrote.[10]

Eyewitness

But when did the authors originally write the New Testament? After all, it doesn't just matter how close the manuscripts that we have are to when they were originally written, but it also matters how soon the original texts were written after the events that they describe. If too much time has elapsed, then the historical accuracy of the event diminishes and the likelihood of legend creeping in increases. Do we have evidence that the Gospels and New Testament letters were written soon after the events?

First, there are surviving fragments from the Gospels that date to the first century. This alone proves that the gospels must have already been written within a generation after Jesus' life and crucifixion, which scholars agree was in either AD 30 or 33. However, there is also evidence that the originals were written no more than 20 to 40 years after that date. Unlike today, the authors of antiquity did not sign and date their work. However, they did leave clues that we can use to date the text. For example, because the New Testament does not mention anything about the destruction of the temple in AD 70, or anything about the Roman-Jewish war that led up to its destruction, the gospels and most of the letters must have been written before then. That they would have been written afterward and just not mention the destroyed temple is unthinkable; it would be like a book on modern Jewish history not even mentioning the Holocaust.[11] It just wouldn't make sense not to include this significant event, especially considering that Jesus prophesied that the temple would be destroyed.[12] It would have been advantageous to show that Jesus' prophecy was correct, and yet they don't. The only reasonable conclusion is that it hadn't happened yet.

Further evidence of the early dating of the New Testament is demonstrated by the fact that the text only mentions the death of one of the disciples, James the brother of John, which occurred in AD 44.[13] Consider that the book of Acts is a history of the early church, yet it doesn't mention the death of more well-known disciples such as Jesus' brother James or Peter. Yet, even Josephus records the death of Jesus' brother James as occurring in AD 62. Again, the writers of the New Testament naturally would have included such an important event as the martyrdom of Jesus' brother, but they don't. In fact, they don't even include the death of the Apostle Peter, a prominent figure in the New Testament, which occurred around AD 64. The only reasonable explanation for this is that both James and Peter were still alive when Acts was written. Consider that virtually all scholars acknowledge that the Gospel of Mark was the first Gospel to be written, and that Luke and Acts, essentially two parts of the same book, were written afterward. It follows that if James and Peter are still alive in Luke/Acts, these documents were most likely written before AD 62, which means that Mark must have been written at least a few years prior to that, which is getting incredibly close (within 30 years) to the date of the crucifixion.

An important question to consider is not merely when the New Testament was written, but also when the story of the resurrection of Jesus began to be told. Again, there is good reason to believe that the story of the resurrection was spreading shortly after the event. The Apostle Paul shares a traditional Christian creed that he received from the original disciples, most likely during his visit to Jerusalem sometime between AD 30 and AD 36. This creed dates as one of our earliest sources of what Christians were teaching about the resurrection immediately after it was said to have occurred. The creed, found in 1 Corinthians 15:3-8, says:

> For what I received I passed on to you as of first
> importance: that Christ died for our sins according to
> the Scriptures, that he was buried, that he was raised
> on the third day according to the Scriptures, and that
> he appeared to Cephas [Peter], and then to the Twelve.
> After that, he appeared to more than five hundred of
> the brothers and sisters at the same time, most of whom
> are still living, though some have fallen asleep. Then he
> appeared to James, then to all the apostles, and last of
> all he appeared to me also, as to one abnormally born.

Here, in the earliest creed we have, the facts about the death
and resurrection of Jesus are laid out explicitly. Historians know
that it takes at least two full generations, from 50 to 80 years,
for legend to arise and distort central historical facts.[14] Yet, in
the case of the New Testament, simply not enough time had
elapsed between the actual events of the resurrection and the
original Gospel manuscripts being written for legend to creep
in. Since it was circulating so early, it would have been subject
to the scrutiny of eyewitnesses who were still alive. It's doubtful
that the disciples would have made this story up because the
other eyewitnesses could have discredited the writers' account.
They would have been especially inclined to do so with so grand
a claim as the resurrection of Jesus, had it been false. More than
that, Paul describes returning to Jerusalem many times to meet
with Peter, John, and James in order to make sure that he had
the details of the story correct.[15] As the Apostle Peter writes,
"For we did not follow cleverly devised stories when we told you
about the coming of our Lord Jesus Christ in power, but we were
eyewitnesses of his majesty."[16]

Promise Keeper

Not only was the New Testament written too early to be a myth, but also it doesn't read as a legend; it doesn't sound like something that a bunch of Jewish fishermen would make up. In order to understand this point, it is important to review some of the background history of the Jews, since this history helps explain the worldview within which the disciples were operating.

As Jews, the disciples would have understood themselves to be God's chosen people, the people of Israel, for whom God had promised to protect and care. They saw themselves in a grand narrative that involved alternating cycles of freedom and slavery, with God rescuing them each time and instituting reminders of the promises that he had made and that he had kept. The first enslavement began in the Garden of Eden when Adam and Eve's disobedience caused all of creation to become enslaved to sin and evil. However, even then, at the very beginning, God had a plan to rescue his people. As a reminder of this, God later instituted the Day of Atonement, *Yom Kippur*, when the Jewish High Priest would sacrifice a spotless animal for the sins of the nation to be forgiven. This day served not only as a reminder that they were enslaved to sin, but also as a foreshadowing of what God would do in the future to fulfill his promise and rescue them permanently.

The next series of enslavements were physical captivities caused by their spiritual rebellion. The people of Israel were driven from their land in the same way that Adam and Eve were expelled from the Garden of Eden. First, they became slaves to the Egyptians and were held captive there for 430 years before God, through the leader Moses, led them to freedom. This victory is celebrated in the Jewish festival of Passover.

The next enslavement was to the Assyrians. The twelve tribes of Israel had divided into two kingdoms, the ten northern tribes of Israel and the two southern tribes of Judah. The Assyrians conquered and destroyed the northern kingdom of Israel and took the people captive, but God protected a remnant, the southern kingdom of Judah. Then came the Babylonians, who not only enslaved the southern kingdom of Judah, but also destroyed their temple. The temple was the centerpiece of Jewish religious life and the very place where God lived and where the people worshipped and sacrificed to him.

Seventy years after the temple's destruction, the Jews were released from Babylon. They slowly returned to their land and rebuilt the temple. However, the Jews did not return to their land as free people. They were now under Persian rule. They remained under the control of the Persians until they were conquered by the Greeks, followed by the Ptolemies, and finally the Seleucids. The Seleucid rule however was extremely oppressive; they even began to use the Jewish temple to worship and sacrifice to their own gods. This defilement of the temple was too much for the Jews and they revolted. Under the leadership of the Maccabees, the Jews fought against the Seleucids and won their freedom, leading to the cleansing of the temple. This victory and cleansing of the temple is celebrated in the Jewish festival of Hanukkah.[17]

The Jews were free for a little over a hundred years until, in 63 BC, they were conquered by the Romans. When the Romans took control, they allowed the Jews to self-govern as long as they kept the peace and paid their taxes. When they failed to do so, the Romans put a military ruler or prefect into power.[18] Pontius Pilate happened to be the prefect over Jerusalem at the time of Jesus' arrest and trial. Both Philo and Josephus, first century Jewish writers, indicate that Pilate's rule, like many before and after him, was characterized by corruption, violence, and murder.

Suffering at the hands of the Romans encouraged the Jews to look for a leader like Moses—a Messiah, who would lead the people to freedom. This would have been the mindset of many first century Jews, including the disciples that followed Jesus. Many times their people had been in bondage before, and every time God had rescued them. They were understandably eager for God to rescue them again.

Unlikely King

With this background in mind, it is worth reconsidering whether the story of Jesus' life, death, and resurrection sounds like a legend. Does it sound like something that these disciples, or any other first century Jew, would have been eager to make up? If you wanted to convince yourself and others that Jesus was the Messiah, the promised rescuer sent from God, is this the type of character that would have naturally developed?

Not at all.

Their attention was on Rome. The Jews hated the Romans. They wanted someone, like Moses, appointed by God to be in charge of Israel, who would overthrow the enemy of Rome, and usher in a time of peace and prosperity. That's the type of Messiah that legend would have conjured up.

Instead we have the Biblical Jesus, an anointed leader from God, who gives his winning strategy: defeat? Instead of foretelling a victorious battle, he prophesies his own death by crucifixion! In fact, he wouldn't even fight, but rather, willingly gave himself up to the enemy. It was unthinkable. They wanted a Messiah like Moses, who went into Pharaoh's court with the full power of God and demanded freedom! Instead, God's anointed was to die on a Roman cross? For the Jews, being hanged on a tree or a cross was the worst death imaginable because it was a sign that you were cursed by God.[19]

The Bible tells us that Jesus' plan didn't make any sense to the disciples. From their perspective, Jesus was speaking of defeat before the battle had even begun! This is why, after hearing Jesus prophesy his own death and resurrection, Peter refused to accept it. Matthew 16:22-23 says:

> Peter took him aside and began to rebuke him. "Never, Lord!" he said. "This shall never happen to you!" Jesus turned and said to Peter, "Get behind me, Satan! You are a stumbling block to me; you do not have in mind the concerns of God, but merely human concerns."

You see, Peter wanted to defeat Rome.

But Jesus wanted to defeat evil.

While the Jews were focused on their enslavement to the Romans, Jesus was focused on bringing freedom from life's first enslavement—the one that began in the Garden of Eden. His mission was not to defeat the enemy of Rome, but to defeat life's greatest adversary, evil, and to free people from the death it brings. Jesus came to set the captives free, so that they could live for the purpose they were created for—eternal relationship with God.[20]

Yet, even though Jesus told them what would happen, the disciples still didn't understand Jesus' plan or the enemy he spoke of. Crucifixion was the last thing the disciples expected for their king. When Jesus was arrested, Peter was utterly devastated and demoralized. So, he rejected Jesus and ended up fulfilling

Christ's prediction that he would deny Jesus three times. In fact, Jesus was rejected and abandoned by all of his followers. They witnessed their friend, teacher, and king willingly suffer a terrible death.

Don't Write That!

This is not the type of story that first century Jews would have conjured up, either intentionally or unintentionally. Likewise, the Gospels do not read as a legend. Normally, when we tell a story, we subtly embellish it in order to present ourselves in the best possible light. However, the Gospels tend to do the opposite containing many shameful and embarrassing details: Peter denied Jesus three times, Judas sold Jesus out, and all twelve disciples abandoned Jesus at his arrest and crucifixion. Later the disciples went into hiding because they were so terrified. For a Rabbi, it would not have been a flattering testimony if your devoted students behaved this way. As if that wasn't bad enough, it is Jesus' female followers, instead of the men, that find the empty tomb. In the first century, women were considered less credible than men and did not qualify as legal witnesses.[21] If you were making up a story and wanted it to be credible, you certainly would have men find the empty tomb. Even Jesus' burial contains strange details. For example, the Gospels tell us that Jesus was placed in the tomb of Joseph of Arimathea, a member of the Jewish ruling council called the Sanhedrin. Yet, the early Christians would have viewed the Sanhedrin as partly responsible for Jesus' murder and it would have been disadvantageous to their story to have Jesus associated with someone like Joseph.

These are not the kind of details one would include unless they really happened that way and you were seeking to give an accurate account. That is exactly how the resurrection narrative reads. It reads as history.

One Eighty

But what about the resurrection specifically? Maybe the account of the life of Jesus isn't a legend, but the supernatural elements, such as the miracles and the resurrection, were added in later because of wishful thinking?

By far, the most persuasive reason not to believe that the resurrection arose as a legend is the nature of the belief itself. For first century Jews, the idea of a Messiah rising from the dead before God's return was unthinkable. In their culture, some people, particularly the Pharisees, taught that at the end of the world the dead would be raised to new life, and so Jews collected the bones of deceased loved ones into stone boxes called ossuaries to await this resurrection. However, as Theologian Craig Evans notes:

> Jews who believed in resurrection thought in terms of a general, [end times] resurrection, not the resurrection of an individual. The claim that Jesus was resurrected would have been viewed as problematic, even for his own followers.[22]

So a Messiah that died and then rose again before the end of the world was not something that they expected nor wanted. How would they have even come up with such a belief, let alone desire it to be true?

Further, the ramifications of the resurrection of Jesus changed everything for these Jews—it even changed their very identity. Jewish life and culture was built around following the law of God, which had been given to them at the time of Moses. Yet, because of the resurrection, the disciples completely abandoned their focus on the law and instead committed themselves wholly to the grace found in Jesus Christ. The Apostle Paul says in his letter to the Ephesians, "For it is by grace you have been saved, through faith—and this is not from yourselves, it is the gift of God."[23] This demonstrated a major commitment to Jesus! They were banking everything on Jesus, which marked a radical shift in their worldviews.

It's difficult to believe that something so unthinkably contrary to everything they believed and hoped for could have developed as a legend. The disciples must have witnessed something incredibly real in order to bring about the kind of radical life-change found in the disciples after the resurrection.

Not only did their entire way of thinking about the basics of faith change, but also the very direction and motivation of their lives changed. Consider that those disciples witnessed something after the crucifixion that changed them so radically that it would catapult a movement that would sweep the globe and dominate history. They no longer saw the Romans as enemies, the land of Israel was no longer of interest to them, and observing Jewish law became obsolete. Jesus became their sole focus. What could have caused such a drastic life change? Consider that before the resurrection, the disciples were scared and hiding in a room. Afterward, they became fearless evangelizers who started the world's largest religious movement. History indicates that every single one of them was willing to die for their faith rather than recant. Why would they do that if they had made up the story or they knew that it was a legend? Why suffer and die for a lie that profited them nothing and cost them everything?

This is why virtually all scholars agree that the disciples honestly believed that Christ had been raised from the dead. They were not willingly lying and it was not a legend. As New Testament scholar Gary Habermas says:

> After Jesus' death, the lives of the disciples were transformed to the point that they endured persecution and even martyrdom. Such strength of conviction indicates that they were not just claiming that Jesus rose from the dead and appeared to them in order to receive some personal benefit. They really believed it... If the direct witnesses *really believed* that he rose from the dead, we can dismiss contentions that they stole the body and made up the story. In fact, virtually all scholars agree on that point, whatever their own theological positions.[24]

There are some other facts about the resurrection that all scholars agree on. It is also unanimously acknowledged that both the Apostle Paul and James, the brother of Jesus, started out as unbelievers and were converted after witnessing what they believed was the resurrected Christ. In the case of James, just imagine what it would take to convince you that your brother was not only the King of the Jews, but also the King of Kings, God in the flesh? Anyone with siblings can appreciate how powerful the evidence must have been! Yet, despite starting out as a skeptic, we know that after the resurrection, James became a leader in the Jerusalem church and his faith was so strong that he would eventually be stoned to death for his belief.[25]

In a similar manner, the Apostle Paul started out as an enemy of early Christianity. Saul of Tarsus was a Jew committed to eradicating the Christians, until he encountered the risen Jesus on his way to Damascus and was utterly transformed. Saul, who was also called Paul, committed his life to Jesus, becoming one of the greatest evangelists of all time. Scholars unanimously agree that Paul suffered imprisonment, torture, and beatings for his belief in Jesus.

There is some evidence for the resurrection that just cannot be ignored. Jesus was crucified, the disciples earnestly believed that he had risen from the dead, and the skeptics Paul and James were converted after experiencing the risen Christ. Gary Habermas, in what he called the Minimal Facts Approach, claims that these uncontested facts alone are enough to assert the truth of the resurrection.[26] Basically, his point is that any alternative interpretation has to be able to adequately explain these pieces of evidence. Some have suggested that the disciples lied, that somebody stole the body, that they all experienced a mass hallucination or vision, that Jesus didn't completely die and then revived, that they went to the wrong tomb, or that the resurrection story was simply a variation of myths from other religions. However, none of these suggestions can adequately account for all of the evidence we've looked at. What does satisfy the evidence?

Resurrection.

Any other explanation falls short.

Why the Cross?

But if all this is true—if Jesus really did die on the cross, was buried, and rose again three days later—it makes us ask the question: Why? What did his death and resurrection accomplish? It's important to remember that Jesus had to suffer and die because it was a part of God's plan and fulfilled prophecies written hundreds of years beforehand. One of the most striking prophecies about Jesus is found in Isaiah 53. The Dead Sea Scrolls, which contain the book of Isaiah, are dated to between 335 BC and 100 BC. From them, we read:

> He was despised and rejected by others, and a man of sorrows, and familiar with suffering; and like one from whom people hide their faces and we despised him, and we did not value him. Surely he has borne our sufferings, and carried our sorrows; yet we considered him stricken, and struck down by God, and afflicted. But he was wounded for our transgressions, and he was crushed for our iniquities, and the punishment that made us whole was upon him, and by his bruises we are healed. All we like sheep have gone astray; we have turned, each of us, to his own way; and the Lord has laid on him the iniquity of us all. He was oppressed and he was afflicted, yet he did not open his mouth; like a lamb that is led to the slaughter, as a sheep that before its shearers is silent, so he did not open his mouth...Therefore will I allot him a portion with the great, and he will divide the spoils with the strong; because he poured out his life to death, and was numbered with the transgressors; yet he bore the sins of many, and made intercession for their transgressions.[27]

In this passage, it is easy to see clear details that point to Jesus and how his death gives us forgiveness for sins. But again it makes us wonder: why? Couldn't God just forgive people for the evil they have done? Why did he need to suffer and die?

Think about that question like this: Imagine you are speeding along the freeway, when suddenly, you are pulled over by a police officer. As you are sitting on the side of the road, waiting for the officer to come to your window, a friend who is sitting in the passenger seat looks at you and says, "I forgive you for speeding and, although you broke the law, I'll let it go this time." What would you say? Besides being annoyed, you'd just ignore him and continue to wait for the officer because you know that you have just broken the government's law, not your friend's law. Only the government can forgive that offense. For this reason, it is important to remember that Jesus claimed to be God; only he had the authority to forgive us for breaking God's laws, the law that is above man's law.

Now imagine that as the officer approaches your car, you roll down the window and begin to explain that you can't receive a speeding ticket because you're a good person. You pay your taxes, volunteer regularly, and of course, this is your first time speeding.

Yeah, right.

We all know that doing good deeds, as great as they may be, do not amend broken laws. In fact, a government that allowed you to get out of broken laws by doing "good deeds" would not be a "good" government—it would be corrupt. Why then is it that something we would never expect from our government is the very thing that we often plead for from God. If we don't want our governments to be corrupt, why would we want God to be? God is not corrupt, nor is he even corruptible.

The reality is, when we get pulled over for speeding, we are at the mercy of the police officer or judge. Although we all appreciate being shown mercy, mercy alone is not good. Imagine a government that only showed mercy, giving out warnings every time the law was broken: we would end up crying out for justice. The same is true of a government that never shows mercy. Imagine a nation that prosecuted every offense to the full extent of the law: the people would begin to cry out for mercy.

It's important to realize that God is perfect in both his justice and his mercy. God is completely holy. The word "holy" means "separate"; he is completely other from us in his perfection. In comparison to God, the evil of this world is disgustingly vile and demands justice. This is true not only of the evil that has been done to us, but also of the evil, or sin, that we have done to others; the reality is that we are all guilty of much more than speeding and find ourselves under God's justice. Yet thankfully, God also abounds in mercy and lavishes us with his loving kindness. How then could a holy God display perfect justice, in light of his loving mercy?

The cross.

The Cost of Grace

On the cross is where God's perfect justice and mercy are satisfied. As Jesus hung by the nails in his hands and feet, God poured out his justice on Jesus instead of on us. Through the cross, Jesus demonstrates the depths of God's mercy by taking our place. Quoting the prophecy from Isaiah 53, the Apostle Peter says:

> When they hurled their insults at him, he did not retaliate; when he suffered, he made no threats. Instead, he entrusted himself to him who judges justly. 'He himself bore our sins' in his body on the cross, so that we might die to sins and live for righteousness; 'by his wounds you have been healed.'[28]

Jesus was punished on the cross for *our* evil. What was that penalty? It was the worst penalty possible: separation from his heavenly Father. Have you ever noticed how people are punished in our culture? If you disobey your mom, you go for a time out. If you disobey the government, you go to jail. If you misbehave in jail, you're put into solitary confinement. Even the hardest criminal is a testament to the truth that the worst punishment we can imagine is to be denied relationship with others. The punishment for evil is separation from God, which Jesus willingly took in our place. As Jesus died on the cross, he cried out, "My od, my God, why have you forsaken me?"[29] At that moment, as he took the punishment of evil in our place, he was denied relationship with God the Father.

The result is that through Jesus' sacrifice, we are able to receive something far greater than justice and mercy: grace.

Simply put, justice is getting what you deserve: death.

Mercy is not getting what you deserve: forgiveness.

Grace is getting something good that you don't deserve: relationship.

Justice and mercy can be seen in this example: It is like heading to court to pay the speeding ticket that you rightly deserve, but instead of receiving a fine, the judge pays it for you! Justice has been served and mercy has been shown. You are now free to go. However, Christianity is not about God just setting us free to go; in that case we would still not be fulfilling the purposes we were created for. Rather, it's about reconciling us back to himself. Through Christ's work on the cross, we are free to come to God because we have received Christ's perfect relationship with God. That's how much God loves you. It's like the judge not only paying your speeding ticket, but then exchanging your blemished driving record for his perfect one.

Got Hope?

The cross showed God's perfect justice, mercy, and grace—but the resurrection demonstrated Jesus' power to accomplish it. The resurrection gives us confidence that Jesus was telling the truth and that his death saves us from evil and the death it brings. The resurrected Jesus *is* the hope of eternal life.

But what does eternal life look like? It's important to note that the resurrection was much more than just a supernatural miracle. New Testament scholar N.T. Wright explains that the resurrection was more than just Jesus being brought back from the dead, to the same type of life he had before, as if death had just been postponed. Rather, in his book, *The Resurrection of the Son of God*, he writes:

[Resurrection] always means *transformation*, going through the process of death and out into a new kind of life beyond, rather than simply returning to exactly the same sort of life...[The Christian] looks forward to eventual bodily resurrection, to a new body which will have left behind the decay and corruption of the present one, and which will function in relation to present life like a new and larger suit of clothes to be put on over the existing ones.[30]

Jesus didn't just regain the life he'd had before; instead, he was the first example of a whole new type of life that would come after being dead—eternal life with God! While the disciples did witness Jesus defeat death, they also witnessed more than that—death's complete reversal. Jesus would never die again. He was a physical demonstration, living proof, that there is eternal life that will come after death. He had a new, resurrected body in which death and disease were defeated forever. The New Testament historian Gary Habermas puts it beautifully:

Jesus's resurrection is an actual *example* of our eternal life. It is the only miracle that, by its very nature, indicates the reality of the afterlife. As Jesus appeared to his followers, heaven had actually broken into the earthly realm. The simplest way to understand the disciples' experience is that the person standing in front of them was walking, talking eternal life. Eternal life was a reality. Since Jesus lives forever, so will believers.[31]

Just like we don't fully know what the reality of hell will be like, we don't fully know what the reality of our new bodies and heaven will be like. What we do know is that eternal life is all about right relationship with God. This hope of new life with God is not something that only affects the future; rather, it should affect how we live in this world right now. C.S. Lewis, put it this way:

> These small and perishable bodies we now have were given to us as ponies are given to schoolboys. We must learn to manage: not that we may some day be free of horses altogether but that someday we may ride bare-back, confident and rejoicing, those greater mounts, those winged, shining and world-shaking horses which perhaps even now expect us with impatience, pawing and snorting in the King's stables.[32]

While we do not yet have resurrected bodies like Jesus, we can already be living with our ultimate purpose in mind. We were made for relationship with God, and we should already be living that way now, as we wait for the wonderful day when that relationship will reach its completion.

Conclusion

That day along the shores of Galilee with Wesley was a powerful reminder of the hope we have in the living Jesus. Wesley wasn't bitter or angry. Instead, I witnessed in him the courage and trust only hope in Jesus can provide in the face of death. There on the shores of the lake, my wife and I watched as Wesley's family tearfully said goodbye to him. This was the end of their vacation and the spot in which they had planned to say their final goodbyes. Soon they would be flying back to their various homes and immersed in work and life again. As my wife and I watched this family say goodbye to their child, brother, and grandson we were reminded that originally the world was not meant to experience death. God loves you and does not want to say goodbye; that's what propelled Jesus to the cross—so that one day when we leave this temporal dwelling, our heavenly father and family can welcome us home. As Wesley's family wept, hugged, and prayed together, it was clear that they were not truly saying "Goodbye." Rather, because of their hope in Jesus, they were actually saying "See you later!"

After the resurrection, Peter and the disciples preached this message of hope to the world. When Peter preached his first sermon, the entire theme of it was that Jesus fought evil and won. Peter quoted a Psalm saying:

> Therefore my heart is glad and my tongue rejoices;
> my body also will rest in hope,
> because you will not abandon me to the realm
> of the dead,
> you will not let your holy one see decay.
> You have made known to me the paths of life;
> you will fill me with joy in your presence.[33]

Because of God's holiness, there is hope that the atrocities of this life will see justice. Through the cross, there is hope that those who call on the name of the Lord Jesus will find mercy from the evil that we are all guilty of. The reality of the resurrection gives us hope that God's grace is sufficient to restore us to real life—relationship with God that starts now and never ends.

Billy Graham has told a fascinating story of a time when he met with the West German Chancellor, Konrad Adenauer. In the middle of their conversation, Adenauer paused and asked Billy Graham this question: "Mr. Graham, do you really believe that Jesus Christ rose from the dead?" Billy Graham, somewhat taken aback by the question, said, "Sir, if I did not believe in the resurrection of Jesus Christ, I would have no gospel left to preach." At that, the Chancellor paused, walked over to the end of the room, looked out of the window at the post-war ruins, and said, "Mr. Graham, outside of the resurrection of Jesus Christ, I know of no other hope for mankind."[34]

Do you have hope? Are you facing death like Wesley and Peter did, with confidence that you will spend eternal life with the risen Jesus? Perhaps the most persuasive evidence of all for the resurrection is that you can meet the risen Jesus yourself. You can have a personal relationship with the author of life now. Find out for yourself if Jesus is who he claimed to be.

I did, and it changed my life.

Jesus changed not only they way I viewed God, but also the way I viewed people. I hope it has become clear that the answers we have studied to life's biggest questions are not merely an intellectual exercise. A relationship with God affects the way that we live and love. So, in the last chapter, we will conclude our study of Jesus' answer to the meaning of life by asking what a relationship with God looks like.

Chapter Six

Becoming a Student

I'll never forget the day I met my friend Chris. I had just returned from my second trip to Calcutta, India, where I had led a team of six people to serve at Kalighat for three weeks. While giving a presentation at church, I shared about the trip and challenged people to serve God wherever he leads them. After the service, Chris came and introduced himself to me. He was clearly moved by what I had said and excited to serve God. He asked me about joining an upcoming trip to Guatemala that I was leading. We didn't know it at the time, but this would be the start of a friendship that would profoundly impact us both.

As Chris began to share his story with me, I learned that we'd had a similar upbringing. Not only had we both come from broken families, but also, when we were teenagers, we had both attempted to answer the question of life's meaning with drugs and alcohol. Yet, this is where our lives had taken drastically different turns. Three years into that dark valley of my life, I gave up on drugs and alcohol and began to seek life's meaning elsewhere. That journey would eventually bring me to God and, then later, to Jesus Christ. Chris, however, had not given up on drugs and alcohol. Instead, he had descended into a cycle of narcotic highs and ever-deeper lows. Finally, after sixteen years, he reached the valley floor. Only when he was homeless, friendless, and feeling worthless, did he decide to find his meaning elsewhere. Chris went into recovery, eventually joining Psalm 23 Transition Society, a transition house, to help him get back on his feet.[1]

Chris was in this transition house when I met him. He had recently discovered the meaning of life in Jesus, but he needed help. He didn't fully understand what that looked like. So, Chris asked if I would help him follow Jesus.

In the church, we call someone who follows Jesus a disciple. In fact, the word "disciple" means "student." Philosopher and Christian thinker Dallas Willard (1935-2013) wrote, "A disciple is a learner, a student, an apprentice—a *practitioner*, even if only a beginner."[2] The Apostle Paul understood that becoming a good student is easier if you have someone modeling it for you. That's why he told the church in Corinth, "Follow my example, as I follow the example of Christ."[3] This type of apprenticeship is the same thing that we do when learning a career. Yet, what many of us don't realize is that the Christian life is no different. Chris wanted to be a disciple of Jesus, but in order to do that, he needed to apprentice.

Chris and I began to meet weekly, sometimes even twice a week. We would go for walks together and talk about faith and life. He would join my wife and me for dinner and play with our kids—he became part of our family. He was also part of a much larger family: the church. Chris not only attended our church regularly, but also was actively involved in the church, volunteering wherever needed. There were many other men in our church that were invested in Chris as well.

After two years of mentoring Chris, my family and I moved from Abbotsford, British Columbia, to Los Angeles, California, so I could complete my master's degree at Biola University. Chris helped me drive a U-Haul down to California and move into my apartment, while my wife flew down with the kids. A few weeks after Chris returned to Canada, I was shocked to learn that he had been hospitalized. For no apparent reason, one of his lungs had suddenly collapsed. Thankfully, Chris survived, but the battle wasn't over; instead, he was about to face the greatest challenge of his life. A year earlier, Chris had been hit by a car and was just now receiving a settlement check from the insurance company. That sudden influx of cash would prove to be much more dangerous than a spontaneously collapsed lung. I was furious when I learned that Chris had used the money to purchase cocaine—a lot of cocaine. He locked himself into a sleazy motel and began to binge.

To my shame, my first response was anger.

I was angry that Chris had wasted two years of *my* life! All the time and effort I had invested in him was gone and we would need to start over. That was assuming that Chris even wanted to try again. I didn't. His life was too messy and I didn't want him to waste any more of my time with him. What assurance did I have that he wouldn't relapse again?

So, I wrote him off.

Finding Grace

In the Gospel of Luke, we read about a time when a teacher of the Jewish law stood up to question Jesus' teaching: "Teacher," he asked, "what must I do to inherit eternal life?" Jesus, in characteristic fashion, responds with a question: "What is written in the Law? How do you read it?" The teacher of the law replies, "Love the Lord your God with all your heart and with all your soul and with all your strength and with all your mind; and, love your neighbor as yourself." Essentially, the man confirms Jesus' teaching on the meaning of life: love God and love people. The man had answered well and Jesus affirms him, replying, "You have answered correctly. Do this and you will live."[4]

It sounds so simple: we will have eternal life if we just love God and love other people. Yet, the problem is that we don't do this. We can't! We may try to love God and we all love some people, but we don't love everyone and those we do love, we don't love perfectly all the time. The law is really helpful at showing us how incapable we are of obeying it. Sooner or later, this becomes apparent in all of our lives. Jesus is constantly trying to push us past paying mere lip-service to the law, to help us realize that we need someone who can obey the law for us, someone whose righteousness we can rely on instead of our own.

Yet, instead of relying on him, we like to do things in our own strength and, if that doesn't work, to justify our actions. The teacher's response to Jesus is interesting because he does something that we all do; in his inability to keep God's law, he tries to find a way out. He thinks that by changing the definitions a little, by subtly tweaking the nuances of the law, that he can find a loophole and justify himself. So, he asks Jesus, "And who is my neighbor?"

It's helpful to know that this was a common question at the time; there was a debate going on as to who exactly counted as a neighbor. According to many Jewish leaders, certain groups had become excluded from the love command. Most Jews excluded Samaritans, foreigners, and resident aliens who did not convert within a year.[5] In other words, the man was looking for Jesus to confirm which people he *didn't* need to love. Then he would have his loophole, his justification.

Jesus answers his question by telling the now-famous parable of the Good Samaritan, a title that has become synonymous with good deeds. In the parable, a man is travelling the road from Jerusalem to Jericho when he is attacked by robbers.[6] The man is lying half-dead and naked on the side of the road when three people pass him by. The first person to pass by is a priest. Even though the priest is theoretically one of the most righteous people in all of Jewish culture, he doesn't stop when he sees the man in need of help and even crosses to the other side of the road in order to avoid him. The second person is a Levite, a priest's assistant, and he too goes to the other side of the road, leaving the man to die alone. The third person to pass by is a Samaritan, a member of the group most hated by the Jews. Contrary to expectation, instead of ignoring him like the others have done, the Samaritan stops and bandages the man up. In fact, the Samaritan goes out of his way to take the man to an inn and pay for him to be taken care of until he has fully recuperated.

As you can imagine, this story would have been scandalous to Jesus' listeners. A Samaritan was the last person they expected to out-do a priest or a Levite. Samaritans were among the least respected of all people groups; they were considered unclean and to be avoided at all costs. It would be as if a carjacking took place in your neighborhood and a pastor ignored the whole thing but a drug dealer stopped to help.

Jesus ends the parable by asking, "Which of these three do you think was a neighbor to the man who fell into the hands of robbers?" The expert in the law replied, "The one who had mercy on him." Jesus told him, "Go and do likewise."[7]

The point of Jesus' story is simple: your neighbor is anyone in need. People who truly love God will show mercy to those in need. Jesus said, "You have heard the law that says, 'Love your neighbor' and hate your enemy. But I say, love your enemies! Pray for those who persecute you! In that way, you will be acting as true children of your Father in heaven."[8] The point is not to be on the lookout for who we do not need to serve, but instead to be attentive to who we *can* serve, no matter who they are or whether they have earned it or not.

Still a Student

If there is one thing I have learned on my journey with God, it is that he always has something to teach me, especially when I think that I have it all figured out. As I reflect on this teaching and on my relationship with Chris, I realize how often I misunderstand Jesus. For a good portion of my life, I have viewed myself as the Good Samaritan in the story, as though Jesus told the story just to remind me of how great I am. Yet, after I wrote Chris off, I was in turmoil. I wanted to ignore the man half-dead on the side of the road, but God wouldn't let me. Truth is, most days, I'm not the Good Samaritan in the story—instead, I'm the teacher of the law trying to justify myself. It's in moments like these that I'm reminded that I too am a student of Jesus, with much to learn.

Originally, I had thought that my relationship with Chris was all about what *he* needed to learn. In the days following the news of Chris' relapse, God began to show me what *I* needed to learn. I had the whole "meaning of life" answer down pat, just like that teacher of the law, but I was struggling to practice it. Although I had been shown grace, I was graceless to others. I had subconsciously convinced myself that I had earned God's grace.

Clearly, I didn't fully understand grace.

After a good long look into my own issues, I began to do what I should have done from the beginning: I stopped to help. I began by praying for Chris. Then, I called him. It took some work convincing him to even take my call, but he finally did. I told him that God still loved him and that I loved him too. Although I couldn't make the right choices for him, I would still be his friend and I would be there for him, no matter what. Since I was still in Los Angeles, I contacted one of our friends from church and together, we convinced Chris to give us his wallet. That was all we could do.

The rest would be up to Chris. Although he had been shown grace, he felt unworthy to receive it. He had been trying to earn God's grace and, in the process, had become prideful in his accomplishments. He was ripe for a fall. Now, he sat in that motel room with a pile of cocaine and a decision to make.

I'll let Chris tell the story from his own perspective.

Chris' Perspective

It's funny, but I'll never forget my first meeting with Andy either. I had seen him around during the three months that I had been attending church, but I had never said hello. This changed, however, during his presentation and sermon about the trip to Calcutta. I remember feeling the presence of God so closely that tears came to my eyes. It seemed clear to me that the next step in my spiritual growth was to leap out and do something radical. So, I introduced myself to Andy and explained that I was interested in traveling with him on his next mission trip, which happened to be to Guatemala. I had already been meeting informally with various men from the church, but I was interested in a deeper spiritual maturity that I had witnessed in others. From reading the New Testament, and gauging from the little experience that I had, I knew that this would take intentionality and time. So, I asked Andy to mentor me. The rest, as they say, is history.

We started to meet every week, usually taking his son Tristan to the park. Along the way, we would discuss everything from the meaning of life, to the resurrection of Christ, to what constitutes a robust worldview. He gave me books to read. He challenged my faith and taught me to defend it. During this time, Andy truly invited me into his life. This undoubtedly had the biggest impact on me, as it helped show me what real meaning looks like when it is lived out.

The search for meaning had always been an important thing in my life. In the past, I had sought it out, but to no avail. At age thirteen, my life went sideways and I became an alcoholic and a drug addict. I was just trying to provide meaning to an otherwise meaningless life, or to forget it all together. I just wanted to extinguish the pain I felt inside. For sixteen years, I was a mess of emotion gone awry, a passionate self-destruction. This life was without meaning, I supposed, and who could tell me otherwise?

After some time living this way, I came to a crossroads. There's a quotation I remembered from the movie The Shawshank Redemption, in which the inmate Andy says, "I guess it comes down to a simple choice really, get busy living or get busy dying." The peculiar thing at this point in my life was that, for some reason, I felt that living was the better option. What could have possibly given me this notion? I now believe that it was God's revelation, through both nature and some lovely people. I came to think that life indeed contained meaning, and that I needed to seek out the giver of it. This led me to God and the wonderful life I now live with Jesus.

I wish I could say that I just trailed off into the sunset with Jesus, the final frame of my life saying, "They all lived happily ever after." But life doesn't always work out that way. In late 2009, after getting run down by a car and then experiencing a spontaneous pneumothorax, my poorly looked-after faith failed underneath me. My relapse was sudden and intense. After being nearly two years clean, I spent the better part of six days locked away in a rundown motel with a lot of money, bad company, and an attitude that left much to be desired. This episode seemed as though it had no chance of ending well.

Unbeknownst to me, Andy was going through an incredible struggle of his own as this played out. I had assumed, rightly, that he would be disappointed. I had disappointed just about everyone, by my count. What I didn't know was that the challenge that God was laying at Andy's feet was the grace of Christ in my life. Once the relapse occurred, I had quickly come to the conclusion that I was a dirtbag loser that had no business calling on a holy God for mercy and grace, let alone calling myself a Christian. I still believed God existed; I just didn't think God wanted me. I thought there was no grace for a person like me.

It turns out that my idea of grace was inextricably linked to my perception of self-worth. This thinking clearly demonstrates where I was spiritually. I had developed a faith cobbled together on pride and works—a faithless faith. I had begun to let the concepts of success and acceptance answer the question of meaning in my life. With my relapse, I had obviously failed. So, I avoided those I loved, including God. "Who would want me anyway," I thought. But there in that motel room, I remember sensing the presence of God and being confused. I remembered thinking, "God, you shouldn't be here." Then, I began to realize that he had not given up on me. God had never stopped loving me.

Many visitors came to that motel to help me, even though I turned them all away, and even more prayed. Together, they helped find the chinks in my armor. God's love for me was relentless. Finally, Andy got me on the phone and convinced me to man up and do the right thing. The first step was turning over my access to more money. With that done, I was still left with a lot of cocaine and a brittle will with which to fight temptation. I had a choice to make. By God's good grace, I was able to really sleep for the first time in six days, thus clearing my head a little. When I woke, the strength of God helped me.

I flushed the rest of the crack down the toilet.

Finally, it was time to let my pride go. So, after some encouragement and prayer, I re-entered the same transition house that I had spent seven months in, during my first stint in recovery. I was starting over.

Some of you might be asking: what does this all mean? I really can't tell you. All I can say is how God used it. He used this situation to speak into my life and talk to me about our relationship. C.S. Lewis is noted for saying, "God whispers to us in our pleasures, speaks in our conscience, but shouts in our pains: it is his megaphone to rouse a deaf world."[9] This situation was no different. As a fallen man, the things I hate most are the things that come most naturally to me. It takes a supernatural voice to be heard over them calling out to me.

Amazing Grace

As Chris discovered the depths of God's grace, so did I. I realized that in my brokenness I can be legalistic and graceless, but God still loves me. God wasn't going to give up on me, nor did he want me to give up on Chris. My friendship and love for Chris is no longer based on his successes or failures. Although I don't want Chris to slip up, nor do I want to be used,[10] it's no longer about him or me, it's about God. It's about what God has done for me that inspires me to love people. God put Chris in my path and taught me how to show grace, the same grace that I had received from God. Chris, on the other hand, was learning how to receive grace. I've learned that loving people is never a waste of time; it's what we're meant to do. Although I don't always get it right, I am learning.

This is why church is so important to me. Church is the one place where the fullness of the meaning of life is played out. It's where we gather together as a grace-filled community to love God and learn to love our neighbours. It's a place to hold us accountable when we fail and to inspire us to keep going. It's not difficult to see that the world needs a whole lot more of that. Does the church always get it right? No. But when it does, it's heavenly.

Thankfully, Chris has now been walking with God, free from drugs and alcohol, ever since the relapse. He even went to college to become a pastor and graduated with highest honors. Chris has become a brilliant instrument of God's grace, serving the local church and people around the globe.

While serving in Poland, he met a beautiful girl named Sara who was also serving God with her life. Soon they fell in love. It was one of the great honors of my life to officiate their wedding. I will never forget standing in the back room with Chris, waiting for the service to begin. After praying for Chris, that God would bless their marriage, I noticed tears in his eyes. He looked at me and said, "Andy, as I compare my life with Sara's, I can't help but feel that I don't deserve her." Being the good friend that I am, I quickly responded, "That's because you don't!" As he laughed and dried his tears, I continued, "Chris, that's the beautiful thing about grace. You don't deserve Sara, yet she loves you anyway."

In his letter to the Ephesians, the Apostle Paul reminds us of this, "For it is by grace you have been saved, through faith—and this is not from yourselves, it is the gift of God—not by works, so that no one can boast."[11]

Amazing!

Grace reminds us that we can't earn God's love.

It's a gift.

The truth is, I do not deserve God, and yet, he loves me. You can't earn this love and you can't take it away. It just is. Once you experience this grace, you can't help but be inspired to love others.

Interconnected

If you remember way back to chapter one, we started this journey by looking into Jesus' answer to the meaning of life. Jesus explained that people were created for the purpose of eternal relationship with both God and people. This started us on a journey to see if Jesus' answer is true. In chapter two, we looked through the telescope and the microscope to discover evidence for an author of life, concluding that there are good reasons to believe that God does exist. Naturally, we asked if it was possible to know this God. In chapter three, we learned that although we can't reach God, God can and did reach us in the person of Jesus Christ. All of this led to a significant concern: if God exists and created us for relationship, why is our world so broken? In chapter four, we realized that God did not break relationship with us—people are responsible for that. Through an act of rebellion, people ushered evil into a good world, which ultimately led to the eternal separation of death. This series of questions then climaxed with chapter five, where we explored whether evil, and the death it brings, can be defeated. More than just wondering if there is life after death, we considered whether there is eternal relationship with God after death. Jesus' life, death, and resurrection became the foundation on which all the other questions rest. Because Jesus defeated death, I have good reason to believe that he is who he claimed to be and can provide relational life with God that begins now and never ends. Thus, we have come full circle. Exploring all of these questions has brought us back to the answer of chapter one: we are created to love God but because of sin that relationship can only be restored through a God that loves us.

It's often said that we come into the world with nothing and we leave with nothing. Yet, I hope that throughout this book, you have seen that simply isn't true. You came into the world bearing the image and love of your Creator, and through relationship with God, by the work of Jesus Christ, you can reflect that image in this life.

At the end of 1 Corinthians 13, a famous passage about love, the Apostle Paul writes, "And now these three remain: faith, hope and love. But the greatest of these is love."[12] Paul is reminding us that once we die, we will no longer need our faith and our hope will be fulfilled. The only thing that will remain is the love in which we have lived this life. We are then confronted with this question: Will you love God?

You will never regret living a life that is devoted to loving God and people. After all, that's what you were created for.

It seems fitting to end this book with a prayer that the Apostle Paul wrote for the church he loved in Ephesus. Paul began as a graceless man in search of meaning, until he encountered the love of God found in a risen saviour. Paul became a new person in Jesus. He became one of Jesus' greatest students. His prayer for the church is my prayer for you:

> For this reason I kneel before the Father, from whom every family in heaven and on earth derives its name. I pray that out of his glorious riches he may strengthen you with power through his Spirit in your inner being, so that Christ may dwell in your hearts through faith.

And I pray that you, being rooted and established in love, may have power, together with all the Lord's holy people, to grasp how wide and long and high and deep is the love of Christ, and to know this love that surpasses knowledge—that you may be filled to the measure of all the fullness of God.

Now to him who is able to do immeasurably more than all we ask or imagine, according to his power that is at work within us, to him be glory in the church and in Christ Jesus throughout all generations, for ever and ever!

Amen.[13]

THINKING?

Notes

Chapter One

What is the Meaning of Life?

1. Teahouse-trekking is a very popular style of trekking in Nepal. It involves trekking from one person's home or lodge to another. These teahouses are set up right along the trekking trail and provide food and accommodation.

2. Saint Augustine, *The Confessions of Saint Augustine*, trans. John K. Ryan (New York: Doubleday, 1960), 43.

3. Jim Carrey, Commencement speech at Maharishi University of Management Graduation, May 24, 2014, https://www. mum.edu/whats-happening/graduation-2014/full-jim-carrey-address-video-and-transcript/.

4. Ecclesiastes 2:1-11 NLT.

5. Tom Brady, "Tom Brady: The Winner," interview by Steve Kroft, CBS: 60 *Minutes*, November 6, 2005, http://www.cbsnews.com/news/tom-brady-the-winner/3/ (accessed June 4, 2014).

6. Leo Tolstoy, *A Confession*, trans. David Patterson (New York: W.W. Norton & Company, 1983), 29.

7. Ibid., 30.

8. Theologian Peter Kreeft considers this "argument from desire" to be one of the strongest arguments for God's existence. His formal reasoning goes like this:

   • Premise 1: Every natural, innate desire in us corresponds to some real object that can satisfy that desire.

   • Premise 2: But there exists in us a desire, which nothing in time, nothing on earth, no creature can satisfy.

   • Conclusion: Therefore there must exist something more than time, earth and creatures, which can satisfy this desire. This something is what people call "God" and "life with God forever."

   Peter Kreeft, *The Handbook of Christian Apologetics* (Downers Grove: Intervarsity Press, 1994), 78.

9. C.S. Lewis, *Mere Christianity* (New York: Touchstone, 1996), 121.

10. At this point, it is important to recognize that we are talking about innate desires, rather than artificial desires. Innate desires (like hunger, thirst, tiredness, etc.) are universal

and originate naturally within us – they do not need to be suggested by external sources. On the other hand, artificial desires (the desire to fly, to travel, to own a fancy car, etc.) vary from person to person and have to be culturally conditioned in us by things such as advertising. Therefore, one can't claim the invalidity of the argument by claiming that artificial desires exist which cannot be fulfilled (e.g. the desire to fly cannot be fulfilled in reality). The argument from desire only claims that natural innate desires can be fulfilled in reality. For a greater explanation see: Peter Kreeft, *The Handbook of Christian Apologetics*.

11. Thomas V. Morris, *Making Sense of It All: Pascal and the Meaning of Life* (Grand Rapids: William B. Eerdmans Publishing Company, 1992), 56-57.

12. In the Christian worldview, God created all things. So, in that way, Christians believe that all things, like a rock or a tree, *do* have meaning, because they were given that meaning by the Creator. Any meaning that humans add, such as taking that rock or tree and creating a house, is therefore a secondary meaning, with the primary meaning still being the one given by God. If God is removed from the equation, then all that is left is secondary, or what we call later "subjective" meaning, and there is no ultimate or objective meaning to anything.

13. Morris, 61.

14. Percy Bysshe Shelley, "Ozymandias," in *The Norton Anthology of Poetry*, eds. Margaret Ferguson, Mary Jo Salter, and Jon Stallworthy (New York: W.W. Norton & Company, 1997), 469.

15. I am indebted to Dr. William Lane Craig for pointing out this illustration to me by means of his book *Reasonable Faith.*

16. Friedrich Nietzsche, *The Gay Science,* ed. Walter Kaufmann (New York: Vintage, 1974), 181-82.

17. William Lane Craig, *Reasonable Faith: Christian Truth and Apologetics,* 3rd Ed. (Wheaton: Crossway, 2008), 77.

18. Mark 12:16-17.

19. Mark 12:30-31.

20. Leviticus 19:2.

21. Leviticus 19:18 NLT.

22. John 13:35.

23. 1 John 4:19.

24. I am grateful to my friend Jon for helping me with the phrasing of this point.

25. Saint Augustine, 43.

26. William Van Poyck, "May 12, 2013," *Death Row Diary,* May 18, 2013, http://deathrowdiary.blogspot.ca/2013/05/may-12-2013.html

27. Douglas Coupland, *Life After God* (New York: Washington Square Press, 1994), 359.

28. Tolstoy, 63.

Chapter Two
Does God Exist?

1. Plato, *The Republic of Plato*, trans. A.D. Lindsay (New York: E.P. Dutton & Co, 1957). There is no academic consensus on the exact dating of Plato's life, so the dates I have used are approximate.

2. Aristotle, "Metaphysics," trans. W.D. Ross, *The Internet Classics Archive,* http://classics.mit.edu/Aristotle/metaphysics.html.

3. "The Global Religious Landscape." PEW Research Religion and Public Life Project http://www.pewforum. org/2012/12/18/global-religious-landscape-exec/ [accessed Sept. 8, 2014].

4. Justin L. Barrett, *Born Believers: The Science of Children's Religious Belief* (New York: Free Press, 2012), 3.

5. Plato, 257-264.

6. René Descartes, *Meditations on First Philosophy*, trans. Donald A. Cress (Indianapolis: Hackett Publishing Company, 1993), 13-16.

7. Nick Bostrom, "Are You Living in a Computer Simulation?," *Philosophical Quarterly* 53, no. 211 (2003): 243-255.

8. René Descartes, *Discourse on the Method of Rightly Conducting One's Reason and Seeking Truth in the Sciences*, trans. Jonathan Bennett, http://www.earlymoderntexts.com/pdfs/descartes1637.pdf

9. Psalm 19:1-4a.

10. Actually, I have no idea what it was, but it cost me about $3 to take a look. Undoubtedly, it was money well spent.

11. Physicalism is also commonly denoted by the terms materialism or naturalism, as well as a combination with the word "scientific" (i.e. Scientific materialism, etc.) Philosophers may recognize that these terms do not mean precisely the same thing, but for the majority of writers, the differences are too small to count and the terms are usually used to refer to the same basic worldview principles.

12. *Cosmos*, DVD, starring Carl Sagan (Cosmos Studios, 2002).

13. Biologist George Klein and geneticist Richard Lewontin are two such scientists who admitted that their disbelief in God is *a priori*, a result of their ardent physicalism.

    Klein says: "I am not an agnostic. I am an atheist. My attitude is not based on science, but rather on faith...The absence of a Creator, the non-existence of God is my childhood faith, my adult belief, unshakable and holy."

    Lewontin says: "Our willingness to accept scientific claims that are against common sense is the key to an understanding of the real struggle between science and supernatural. We take the side of science in spite of the patent absurdity of some of its constructs...in spite of the tolerance of the scientific community for unsubstantiated just-so stories, because we have a prior commitment...to materialism. It is not that the methods and institutions of science somehow compel us to accept a material explanation of the phenomenal world but, on the contrary, that we are forced by our a priori adherence to material causes to create an apparatus of investigation and a set of concepts that produce material explanations, no matter how counter-intuitive, no matter how mystifying to the uninitiated."

    As quoted in John C. Lennox, *God's Undertaker: Has Science Buried God?* (Oxford: Lion Hudson, 2007), 34-35.

14. John Hedley Brooke, *Science and Religion* (Cambridge: Cambridge University Press, 2014), 29.

15. Of course, as with any era, the exact dates of the Scientific Revolution are debated, but it is generally believed to have begun with Nicolaus Copernicus in the 1540s and completed with Isaac Newton in the 1680s.

16. Cited in Max Casper, *Kepler,* trans., ed. Doris Hellman (London: Abelard-Schuman. 1954), 381.

17. This has also been the case for Francis Collins, leader of the Human Genome Project. He writes: "The God of the Bible is also the God of the genome. He can be worshipped in the cathedral or in the laboratory. His creation is majestic, awesome, intricate, and beautiful—and it cannot be at war with itself. Only we imperfect humans can start such battles. And only we can end them."

Earlier in the same text, he writes: "for me the experience of sequencing the human genome, and uncovering this most remarkable of all texts, was both a stunning scientific achievement and an occasion of worship."

Francis Collins, *The Language of God* (New York: Free Press Publishers, 2006), 3 & 211.

18. Stephen Jay Gould agrees and asserts that the idea that ancient scholars or explorers believed in a flat earth is a myth. He says: "there never was a period of 'flat earth darkness' among scholars (regardless of how many uneducated people may have conceptualized our planet both then and now). Greek knowledge of sphericity never faded, and all major medieval scholars accepted the Earth's roundness as an established fact of cosmology."

Stephen J. Gould, "The Late Birth of a Flat Earth," in *Dinosaur in a Haystack: Reflections in Natural History* (Cambridge: Harvard University Press, 2011), 42.

19. Draper published *History of the Conflict between Religion and Science* in 1874. In the same year, White published *The Warfare of Science*, a thesis that was subsequently expanded in his *A History of the Warfare of Science with Theology in Christendom* in 1896.

20. James Joseph Walsh, a doctor and contemporary of White, published his response to the conflict thesis in 1908. In it, Walsh says: "The story of the supposed opposition of the Church and the Popes and the ecclesiastical authorities to science in any of its branches, is founded entirely on mistaken notions. Most of it is quite imaginary...Only those who know nothing about the history of medicine and of science continue to harbor it. That Dr. White's book, contradicted as it is so directly by all serious histories of medicine and of science, should have been read by so many thousands in this country...only shows how easily even supposedly educated men may be led to follow their prejudices rather than their mental faculties."

James Joseph Walsh, *The Popes and Science: The History of the Papal Relations to Science During the Middle Ages and Down to Our Own Time* (New York: Fordham University Press, 1908), 19.

21. This is not to say that the advance of science has never incited tension; throughout history, people have been understandably cautious about adjusting their worldview with each new scientific discovery or announcement. This tension has occurred, at times, in both the secular culture and the Christian church. However, the notion that tension

between science and the church is inevitable because of something foundationally irreconcilable between them is pure nonsense. To hold to such a notion is to ignore both the history of science and serious historical scholarship.

22. John Polkinghorne, *Quarks, Chaos & Christianity: Questions to Science And Religion* (New York: The Crossroad Publishing Company, 2006), 116-118.

23. Shalev A. Baruch, *100 Years of Nobel Prizes* (Los Angeles: The Americas Group, 2007), 57-60.

    These percentages include people who identified within the following: Anglican, Baptist, Calvinist, Catholic, Christian, Congregation, Dutch-Mennonite, Dutch-Reform, Eastern Orthodox, Episcopalian, Evangelical, Greek Orthodox, Lutheran, Methodist, Presbyterian, Protestant, Quaker, and Unitarian. In total, people who identified with these Christian groups won 65.4% of all Nobel Prizes during the period of 1901-2000. Atheists, Agnostics, and Freethinkers won just 10.4% of all Nobel prizes in the same period, with the majority being in literature, not science.

24. Peter Atkins, "A New Vision of the Mind," in *Nature's Imagination: the Frontiers of Scientific Vision*, ed. John Cornwell (Oxford: Oxford University Press, 1995), 125.

25. P.B. Medawar, *Advice to a Young Scientist* (New York: Basic Books, 1979), 31 & 101.

26. This estimate is according to the National Aeronautics and Space Administration (NASA). Their Cosmic Distance Scale feature, by Maggie Masetti, gives an excellent picture of just how big space is. http://heasarc.gsfc.nasa.gov/docs/cosmic (accessed August 15, 2014).

27. The project was called the Hubble eXtreme Deep Field (XDF). To read more, visit www.nasa.gov/mission_pages/hubble/science/xdf.html.

28. William Lane Craig and Quentin Smith, *Theism, Atheism and Big Bang Cosmology* (Oxford: Clarendon Press, 1993), 135.

29. "Special Pleading" is a logical fallacy. It is "when someone uses a double standard or argues for an unjustified exception." Nathaniel Bluedorn and Hans Bluedorn, *The Fallacy Detective: Thirty-Eight Lessons on How to Recognize Bad Reasoning* (Muscatine: Christian Logic, 2009), 34.

30. Lee Strobel, *The Case For A Creator: A Journalist Investigates Scientific Evidence That Points Toward God* (Grand Rapids: Zondervan, 2004), 101.

31. William Lane Craig, *Reasonable Faith: Christian Truth and Apologetics*, 3rd Ed. (Wheaton: Crossway, 2008), 154.

32. Lennox, 64.

33. Antonina Vallentin, *The Drama of Albert Einstein* (New York: Doubleday, 1954), 24.

34. Due to problems of classification, sources listing the number of amino acids differ from one another. However, all sources that I consulted recognize between 20–23 amino acids.

35. Michael Denton, *Evolution: A Theory in Crisis* (Chevy Chase: Adler & Adler, 1986), 334.

36. Bill Gates, *The Road Ahead* (London: Penguin, 1996), 228.

37. Some Christians, including Francis Collins, hold to a view called theistic evolution. Though, like all beliefs, it has many varieties, the basic premise is that everything science currently claims about the process of evolution is true, but that evolution has been guided by, and the materials supplied by, God. As Francis Collins says, "Do not fear, there is plenty of divine mystery left. Many people who have considered all the scientific and spiritual evidence still see God's creative and guiding hand at work...For those who believe in God, there are reasons now to be more in awe, not less." Although there is much debate surrounding the topic, theistic evolution does not fall victim to the pitfalls discussed in this chapter the way that unguided, naturalistic evolution does, seeing as theistic evolution acknowledges the need for divine creative power.

Quotation taken from Collins, 106-107.

38. Thomas Nagel, an atheist philosopher, agrees and writes: "In the present intellectual climate such a possibility is unlikely to be taken seriously, but I would repeat my earlier observation that no viable account, even a purely speculative one, seems to be available of how a system as staggeringly functionally complex and informationally-rich as a self-reproducing cell, controlled by DNA, RNA, or some predecessor, could have arisen by chemical evolution alone from a dead environment. Recognition of the problem is not limited to the defenders of intelligent design."

Thomas Nagel, *Mind and Cosmos: Why the Materialist Neo-Darwinian Conception of Nature Is Almost Certainly False* (Oxford: Oxford University Press, 2012), 123.

39. Gunter Knoblich and others, eds., *Human Body Perception from the Inside Out* (Oxford: Oxford University Press, 2006), 3.

40. David J. Charmers, "Facing Up to the Problem of Consciousness," *Journal of Consciousness Studies* 2, no. 3 (1995), 200-219.

41. *The Walking Dead*, Season 1, Episode 6, "TS-19," AMC.

42. Many scientists and philosophers are recognizing the implications of the scientism worldview, and speaking out against the idea that consciousness can be entirely explained in terms of biology. Two important works on this topic are *Mind and Cosmos* by Thomas Nagel and *Aping Mankind: Neuromania, Darwinitis, and the Misrepresentation of Humanity* by Raymond Tallis. Both of these authors are atheists and despite critiquing naturalistic explanations for consciousness, without God, neither are able to offer alternatives.

    Thomas Nagel writes: "Consciousness is the most conspicuous obstacle to a comprehensive naturalism that relies only on the resources of physical science. The existence of consciousness seems to imply that the physical description of the universe, in spite of its richness and explanatory power, is only part of the truth, and that the natural order is far less austere than it would be if physics and chemistry accounted for everything. If we take this problem seriously, and follow out its implications, it threatens to unravel the entire naturalistic world picture." Nagel, 35.

43. Wilder Penfield, *The Mystery of the Mind: A Critical Study of Consciousness and the Human Brain* (Princeton: Princeton University Press, 1975), 76-77.

44. Strobel, 260.

45. Søren Kierkegaard, *Parables of Kierkegaard*, ed. Thomas C. Oden (Princeton: Princeton University Press, 1989), 42.

46. In Christian philosophy, this idea is called epistemic distance. This idea of epistemic distance asserts that God must be far enough away that we have free will, but close enough that we can find him if we so choose.

47. C.S. Lewis, "Is Theology Poetry?" in *The Weight of Glory* (New York: HarperCollins, 2000), 140.

48. In this chapter, we have talked about the cosmological argument and the argument from consciousness, but there are also the teleological, ontological, moral, and fine-tuning arguments, to name a few. See the "Key Resources" section in the reader's guide for more sources on these topics.

Chapter Three

Do All Religions Lead to God?

1. Remember that what we are talking about here are the formal/official teachings of the world's major worldviews. There will always be a difference between these official teachings and the variations of practices embraced by a specific community or individual within that tradition. Because of the variance, some adherents to these worldviews may feel like my summary doesn't do justice to their faith. Although I have tried to be as accurate as possible, this may be an unfortunate result of having to be brief and stick to what the majority in that belief hold as true.

2. Hinduism is incredibly divided on what it means for Brahman to be "personal" or "impersonal." However, even those that would claim that Brahman is personal would not describe Brahman as anything resembling the normally understood concept of a "personal" God who cares for and is involved in individual lives.

3. Dean Halverson, *The Illustrated Guide To World Religions* (Grand Rapids: Bethany House Publishers, 2003), 130-131.

4. Michael Green, *But Don't All Religions Lead to God?: Navigating the Multi-Faith Maze* (Grand Rapids: Baker Books, 2002), 10.

5. Greg Koukl, "The Trouble with the Elephant," Stand to Reason, http://www.str.org/articles/the-trouble-with-the-elephant#.VBtLahbwGFw (accessed September 18, 2014).

6. Paul Copan, *True For You, But Not For Me: Overcoming Objections to Christian Faith* (Minneapolis: Bethany House, 2009), 123.

7. Green, 23-24.

8. The Jehovah's Witnesses are a New Religious Movement (NRM) or cult that was started by a man named Charles Russell in the late nineteenth century. The Jehovah's Witnesses are considered a NRM or cult because they do not hold to the core doctrinal beliefs of orthodox Christianity. Specific to our discussion, they reject the doctrine of the Trinity and do not believe that Jesus is God. Instead, the Watch Tower Society, their governing body which is responsible for all Biblical interpretation and doctrine, teaches that Jesus is God's son, not because he is part of the Trinity, but rather because he was God's first created being through which everything else was made. They believe that Jesus and the archangel Michael are the same being and

that Jesus is not worthy of worship the way that God is. For further reading on this subject, I recommend *Reasoning From the Scriptures with Jehovah's Witnesses* by Ron Rhodes.

9. For some examples, see John 1:1, Philippians 2:6, and Colossians 2:9.

10. Some pronounce it as "Jehovah" instead of "Yahweh," although almost all scholars agree that "Yahweh" is much more likely to be correct.

11. The Masoretic Text, originally written sometime in the seventh century, added notations for where to put the vowels into the Biblical Hebrew text. Most modern translations of the Old Testament rely on this Masoretic Text for accuracy. However, the Masoretic Text makes it very clear that YHWH (called the tetragrammaton) should be treated differently, and notes are usually added in the margins that YHWH should be pronounced *adonai*. Keeping God's name purposefully unpronounceable as a sign of reverence is the reason why many modern Jews will type "G-d" instead of "God." Many modern Bibles will write "LORD" in all-caps in order to indicate spots where the original word is YHWH.

12. Exodus 3:14 KJV.

13. Mark 2:6-7.

14. Mark 2:8-12.

15. Mark 14:61.

16. Mark 14:62.

17. Notice what Jesus says in John 8:58 and how the crowd responds.

18. Mark 14:63-65.

19. Ravi Zacharias, *The Grand Weaver: How God Shapes Us Through the Events of Our Lives* (Grand Rapids: Zondervan, 2007), 82.

20. George Carlin, *You Are All Diseased*, 1999 Eardrum Records, Compact Disc.

Chapter Four

Why is There Evil?

1. Carol Zaleski, "The Dark Night of Mother Teresa," First Things, May 2003, http://www.firstthings.com/article/2003/05/the-dark-night-of-mother-teresa.

2. Sokreaksa S. Himm, *The Tears of My Soul: The Story of a Boy Who Survived the Cambodian Killing Fields* (Oxford: Monarch Books, 2006), 72.

3. Ibid., 106.

4. Bart D. Ehrman, *God's Problem: How the Bible Fails to Answer Our Most Important Question—Why We Suffer* (New York: HarperCollins, 2009), 3-4.

5. Ibid.

6. C.S. Lewis, *Mere Christianity* (New York: Touchstone, 1996), 45.

7. This is the Christian answer to what is called the Euthyphro Dilemma. The classic dilemma, based on one of Plato's dialogues, goes something like this: Is something good because God wills it? Or does God will something because it is good? If it is the first, then morality is at God's whim—if this were the case, he could have arbitrarily declared rape to be good. If it is the second, then morality is independent

of God. However, Christians recognize that the Euthyphro Dilemma is a false dilemma; it doesn't have to be either-or. There is a third option: that God is good by nature and morality is based on his character.

8. J. Budziszewski, *Written on the Heart: The Case for Natural Law* (Illinois: IVP Academic, 1997), 60-61.

9. Martin Luther King Jr., "Letter from Birmingham Jail," April 16, 1963, *The Martin Luther King, Jr. Research and Education Institute at Stanford University*, https://kinginstitute.stanford. edu/king-papers/documents/letter-birmingham-jail.

10. That Hitler didn't know about the Holocaust is one of the main theses in David Irving's book *Hitler's War*, published in 1977. In more recent years, Irving has revised this idea and now claims that there was no Holocaust for Hitler to be ignorant of. The views of Holocaust deniers like Irving are extremely marginalized; all historians agree that the Holocaust was a real historical event and that Hitler had full knowledge of it.

11. Plato held to an idea that has been called Moral Platonism. Basically, he believed that good just existed on its own, as some kind of self-existent idea. However, this idea has been criticized not only for being unintelligible, but also, as I have been arguing, for lacking any kind of obligation on the part of people. If good and evil just exist, then who says that I'm obligated to do good and not evil? Obligation is something you owe to another person. Seashells don't owe you anything, and you don't owe anything to a musical note. But if you borrow a book from a friend, you owe it to him to return it.

The same is true of moral obligation. Once again, we need to have a moral lawgiver—God—in order for morality to exist and for moral obligation to make any sense at all.

12. Romans 2:14-15.

13. Richard Dawkins, *River Out of Eden: A Darwinian View of Life* (New York: Basic Books, 2008), 133.

14. Alex Rosenberg, *The Atheist's Guide to Reality: Enjoying Life without Illusions* (New York: W.W. Norton & Company, 2012), 3.

15. William Lane Craig and Alex Rosenberg, "Is Faith in God Reasonable? William Lane Craig Vs Alex Rosenberg," YouTube Video, 2:47:28, posted by ReasonableFaithOrg, February 6, 2013, www.youtube.com/watch?v=uBTPH51-FoU.

16. Os Guinness, *Time for Truth: Living Free in a World of Lies, Hype & Spin* (Grand Rapids: Baker, 2000), 103.

17. In today's culture, there is a lot of debate surrounding the historicity of Adam and Eve. Some argue that Adam and Eve were real historical figures who were made directly by God and are the biological parents of all humankind. Others insist that Genesis is not interested in scientific explanations and that Adam and Eve are meant to be archetypal figures representing the human condition. Still others espouse a hybrid of any number of these ideas. As interesting as this debate is, it is not especially relevant to our discussion of the origins of evil. Whatever they may believe about the historicity of Adam and Eve, all Christians agree on the original purity of creation and the introduction of evil by the misuse of human and angelic free will. For further reading on this subject, I recommend the book *Four Views On the Historical Adam* published by Zondervan in 2013.

18. Isaiah 55:8-9.

19. Clay Jones, "Ehrman's Problem 5: God Should Intervene More to Prevent Free Will's Evil Use," *Clay Jones* (blog), January 23, 2012, http://www.clayjones.net/2012/01/problem-5-god-should-intervene-more-to-prevent-free-will's-evil-use/.

20. Lewis, *Mere Christianity*, 53.

21. Romans 5:8.

22. Matthew 13:40-42.

23. William V. Crockett, "The Metaphorical View," in *Four Views on Hell*, eds. Stanley N. Gundry and William Crockett (Grand Rapids: Zondervan, 1996), 45.

24. Matthew 5:21-22.

25. Matthew 5:27-28.

26. Romans 3:10-11.

27. Langdon Gilkey, *Shantung Compound: The Story of Men and Women Under Pressure* (New York: HarperCollins Publishers, 1975), 89-92.

28. This is not to say that people never act heroically. People can and do act morally and even take personal risks for selfless motives. A case in point is Eric Liddell, an Olympic champion runner, who was interned in the Shantung Compound with Langdon Gilkey. (For the sake of privacy, he is called "Eric Ridley" in the book.) In the camp, Liddell was consistently shown to be compassionate, generous, and selfless, even suffering a nervous breakdown due to overwork. However, Gilkey makes the point that stories like Liddell's are the exception.

29. Psychological experiments seem to uphold these conclusions, stating that external pressure does not even need to be very high before people start compromising their moral convictions. For examples, research Milgram's Experiments or the Stanford Prison Experiment.

30. Denny Burk, "Rob Bell Outs Himself," *Denny Burk A Commentary on Theology, Politics, and Culture* (blog), February 26, 2011, http://www.dennyburk.com/rob-bell-outs-himself/.

31. Mother Teresa, *A Simple Path* (New York: Random House, 2007), 79.

32. Charles H. Spurgeon, "I Would, But You Would Not," sermon at Metropolitan Tabernacle, Newington, July 22, 1888, *Christian Classics Ethereal Library*, http://m.ccel.org/ccel/spurgeon/sermons40.xl.html.

33. C.S. Lewis, *The Great Divorce* (New York: HarperCollins Publishers, 2001), 75.

34. Jeremiah 17:9.

35. 1 Timothy 2:3-4.

36. Matthew 7:7-8.

37. Genesis 3:15.

38. Himm, 138.

39. Ibid., 126.

40. John 16:33.

41. Romans 8:18.

42. 2 Corinthians 4:17-18.

Chapter Five

Is There Life After Death?

1. Luke 5:1-11.

2. John 21: 22. Italics added.

3. This cultural fascination is evidenced by the number of books in recent years detailing people's near death experiences, many of which have risen to the top of the bestseller lists. My mention of these experiences is not meant to be an endorsement of their authenticity.

4. This is the point the Apostle Paul is making in 1 Corinthians 15:17-19: "And if Christ has not been raised, then your faith is useless and you are still guilty of your sins. In that case, all who have died believing in Christ are lost! And if our hope in Christ is only for this life, we are more to be pitied than anyone in the world." (NLT)

5. Bart D. Ehrman, *Did Jesus Exist? The Historical Argument for Jesus of Nazareth* (New York: HarperCollins Publishers, 2012), 12.

6. Bart Ehrman writes: "The big question is whether a Christian scribe (or scribes) simply added a few choice Christian additions to the passage or whether the entire thing was produced by a Christian and inserted in an appropriate place in Josephus's *Antiquities*. The majority of scholars of early Judaism, and experts on Josephus, think that it was the former - that one or more Christian scribes "touched up" the passage a bit. If one takes out the obviously Christian comments, the passage may have been rather innocuous...It is far more likely that the core of the passage actually does go back to Josephus himself." Ehrman, *Did Jesus Exist*, 60 & 64.

7. Titus Flavius Josephus, *Josephus: The Essential Works: A Condensation of Jewish Antiquities and The Jewish War*, trans. and ed. Paul L. Maier (Grand Rapids: Kregel Publications, 1994), 269.

Contentious parts removed from this version, but present in almost all copies of the *Testimonium Flavianum*, include statements that Jesus *was* the Messiah, that he *did* do miracles, and that he *was* alive after three days, rather than that Jesus' followers only *claimed* these things.

Paul Maier explains his reasoning for trimming the passage of its contested parts and neatly summarizes the various scholarly positions on this issue: "Scholars fall into three main camps: 1) it is entirely authentic; 2) it is entirely a Christian forgery; or 3) it contains Christian interpolations in what was Josephus' authentic material about Jesus. The first option, held by very few, would seem hopeless: no Jew could have claimed Jesus as the Messiah who rose from the dead without converting to Christianity, and Josephus did not convert. The second position, popular in late nineteenth-century skeptical scholarship, has some minor current support. A large majority of scholars today, however, share the third position...Josephus must have mentioned Jesus in authentic core material since this passage is present in all Greek manuscripts of Josephus, and the Agapian version accords well with his vocabulary and grammar elsewhere." Maier, 284.

8. All of the manuscript numbers I use come from a recent article written by Christian thinker Clay Jones for the *Christian Research Journal*. In it, Jones recognizes that people often use incorrect or dated information about manuscript numbers. In an attempt to be as accurate as possible, I have used the updated numbers he has provided.

    Clay Jones, "The Bibliographical Test Updated," *Christian Research Journal* 35, no. 3 (2012).

9. Ibid.

10. William Lane Craig, in his book *Reasonable Faith*, agrees with this conclusion: "In fact, no other ancient work is available in so many copies and languages, and yet all these various versions agree in content. The text has also remained unmarred by heretical additions. The abundance of manuscripts over a wide geographical distribution demonstrates that the text has been transmitted with only trifling discrepancies. The differences that do exist are quite minor and are the result of unintentional mistakes. The text of the New Testament is every bit as good as the text of the classical works of antiquity."

    William Lane Craig, *Reasonable Faith: Christian Truth and Apologetics*, 3rd ed. (Wheaton: Crossway, 2008), 337.

11. This argument only makes sense when you consider just how important the temple was to the entire Jewish nation. The temple was much more than a religious building; rather, it was considered to be the very home of God on earth. The Jews believed that God's presence dwelt in the temple. It was the centre of their entire religious system.

12. Jesus' prophecy of the temple's destruction is recorded in all three synoptic gospels: Matthew 24:1-2, Mark 13:1-2, and Luke 21:5-6.

13. Acts 12:2.

14. A.N. Sherwin-White, *Roman Society and Roman Law in the New Testament* (Oxford: Oxford University Press, 1963), 189-191.

15. Galatians 1:18-20; 2:9.

16. 2 Peter 1:16.

17. The festival of Hanukkah is mentioned in the Bible, in John 10:22, where it is called the Feast of Dedication.

18. Herod the Great became the King of Judea in 37 BC. Although he was called a "King," he was still subject to Roman rule and was required to obey Rome or else lose his position. After his death in 4 BC, his kingdom was subdivided between his three sons: Archelaus was given Judea, Idumaea, and Samaria. The remainder was split between Herod Antipas (Galilee and Peraea) and Herod Philip (Gaulanitis and Trachonitis). However, after only nine years, Archelaus could not keep control of his share of Judea and so the Romans removed him from power and appointed a Roman prefect to rule. Pontius Pilate was the fifth of these prefects.

    Paul Barnett, *Jesus and the Rise of Early Christianity: A History of New Testament Times* (Illinois: IVP Academic, 1999), 109.

19. Deuteronomy 21:23; Galatians 3:13.

20. Isaiah 61:1. In Luke 4:18-21, Jesus confirms that this verse in Isaiah is actually about himself.

21. New Testament scholar and leading authority on the resurrection of Jesus, N.T. Wright, says: "The point has been repeated over and over in scholarship, but its full impact has not always been felt: women were simply not acceptable as legal witnesses. We may regret it, but this is how the Jewish world (and most others) worked...If they could have invented stories of fine, upstanding, reliable male witnesses being first at the tomb, they would have done it. That they did not tells us either that everyone in the early church knew that the women, led by Mary Magdalene, were in fact the first on the scene, or that the early church was not so inventive as critics have routinely imagined, or both."

    N.T. Wright, *The Resurrection of the Son of God, vol. 3* of *Christian Origins and the Question of God* (Minneapolis: Fortress Press, 2003), 607-608.

22. Craig Evans, "Jewish Burial Traditions and the Resurrection of Jesus," *Journal for the Study of the Historical Jesus* 3 (2005): 233-248.

23. Ephesians 2:8-9.

24. Gary R. Habermas and Michael R. Licona, *The Case for the Resurrection of Jesus* (Grand Rapids: Kregel Publications, 2004), 56 & 62.

25. While the death of Jesus' brother James is not mentioned in the New Testament, Josephus records it in his *Antiquities of the Jews*: "Convening the judges of the Sanhedrin, [Ananus] brought before them the brother of Jesus who was called the Christ, whose name was James, and certain others. He accused them of having transgressed the law and delivered them up to be stoned." Although we do not know for certain that James was killed because of his belief in Jesus,

scholars agree that the most reasonable inference is that his leadership in the Jerusalem church was inflammatory enough to have him killed by the Jewish high priest.

Quotation from Josephus, 281.

26. Habermas and Licona, 83.

27. Martin Abegg Jr., Peter Flint, and Eugene Ulrich, *The Dead Sea Scrolls Bible: The Oldest Known Bible Translated for the First Time into English* (New York: HarperCollins Publishers, 1999), 359-360.

28. 1 Peter 2:23-24.

29. Matthew 27:46.

30. Wright, 273 & 368.

31. Gary R. Habermas, *The Risen Jesus & Future Hope* (Lanham: Rowman & Littlefield Publishers, 2003), 163-164.

32. C. S. Lewis, *Miracles* (New York: HarperCollins Publishers, 1996), 266.

33. Acts 2:26-28, quoting Psalm 16:8-11.

34. As quoted in Ravi Zacharias, *The Real Face of Atheism* (Grand Rapids: Baker Books, 2004), 148.

Chapter Six

Becoming a Student

1. Transition homes are for people who, after completing an addictions recovery program, need help transitioning back into regular life again.

2. Dallas Willard, *The Great Omission: Reclaiming Jesus's Essential Teachings on Discipleship* (New York: HarperCollins, 2006), xi.

3. 1 Corinthians 11:1.

4. Luke 10:25-28.

5. Darrell L. Bock, *Luke 9:51-24:53*, vol. 3 of *Baker Exegetical Commentary On The New Testament* (Grand Rapids: Baker Academic, 1996), 1,035.

6. This wouldn't have surprised Jesus' listeners. For a long time, the road from Jerusalem to Jericho had been a well-known haven for bandits. Thievery on that road was common because the terrain in the area was perfect for hiding and making a quick getaway into the wilderness.

7. Luke 10:36-37.

8. Matthew 5:43-45a NLT.

9. C.S. Lewis, *The Problem of Pain* (New York: HarperCollins Publishers, 2001), 91.

10. Please understand this did not mean that I would allow Chris to use me or abuse our relationship. Having clear boundaries with people is very important, especially people in addiction who can be incredibly manipulative. Playing into that harms them more than it helps them. Our goal should always be to help, and sometimes the best way to do that is through tough love. I have seen far too many people who are in an abusive relationship with an addict and think that they are helping, when in fact, they are enabling.

11. Ephesians 2:8-9.

12. 1 Corinthians 13:13.

13. Ephesians 3:14-21.

THINKING?

THINKING?
Answering Life's Five Biggest Questions

READER'S GUIDE

ANDY STEIGER
with sheri hiebert

Reader's Guide

Chapter One

What is the Meaning of Life?

Key Points:

For life to have objective meaning it is necessary to have both of these elements: an author of life and eternal life. Jesus claimed to be the author of life and to be the source of eternal life. Jesus taught that the meaning of life is relationship with God.

Key Questions:

1. What are some of the "mountain peaks" and "valleys" that you've encountered in your life? What's the problem with finding your meaning through "accomplishment climbing"?

2. Why is it that we often assume that famous, successful, or wealthy people have life figured out?

3. Discuss Ecclesiastes 1:1-11. Why is leaving a legacy incapable of giving our lives lasting meaning? Why do you think so many people attempt to find their identity in a legacy?

4. If your name and profession don't define you, what should?

5. If persons are able to give things meaning, why can't we give our own lives meaning?

6. Why did Andy suggest that Jesus is a good place to begin a search for the author of life? Can you think of any other candidates?

7. Explain Jesus' answer to the meaning of life. What do you think about his answer?

8. If Andy is right that the meaning of life is intuitive, why does it often take a "close call" to awaken people to the importance of our relationship with God and people?

Key Scriptures:
- Leviticus 19:18
- Deuteronomy 6:4-9
- Ecclesiastes 1-2
- Mark 12:28-31

Key Resources:
Easy read:
- *Mere Christianity* by C.S. Lewis;
- *The Journey* by Peter Kreeft

Challenging read:
- *Making Sense of It All* by Thomas V. Morris;
- Long Journey Home by Os Guinness

Deep read:
- *Reasonable Faith* by William Lane Craig

Find video resources on this topic at:
- www.thinkingseries.com

Chapter Two
Does God Exist?

Key Points:

Faith is trusting what you have good reason to believe is true. There are good factual and experiential reasons to believe that a relational God exists and that you exist for relationship.

Key Questions:

1. Describe a time in your life when your view of the world was challenged (e.g. when you went to college). How did you reconcile the conflict?

2. Why are both facts and experience important for developing a well-rounded worldview?

3. Why do so many people continue to think that science and Christianity are at war with each other? Are they? Can you believe in God and also be a good scientist?

4. Consider the court case example found in this chapter. How is it possible to be absolutely certain of something without having absolute proof? How does this apply to your belief in the existence of God?

5. Read Psalm 19. What evidence do you find convincing for God's existence?

6. Discuss Zombie Culture. In what ways does dehumanization take place in our culture? How can we eliminate dehumanization?

7. What difference would it make in your life if God either did or did not exist?

8. What do you think of Kierkegaard's story about the king and the maiden? How does Kierkegaard's story make sense of Jesus' teaching on the meaning of life from chapter one?

Key Scriptures:
- Genesis 1-2
- Psalm 19; 139:13-14
- Acts 17:29
- Romans 1:18-23
- Hebrews 3:4; 11:6

Key Resources:
Easy read:
- *The Case for a Creator* by Lee Strobel;
- *The Reason For God* by Timothy Keller

Challenging read:
- *On Guard* by William Lane Craig;
- *God's Undertaker* by John Lennox

Deep read:
- *God and Other Minds* by Alvin Plantinga;

Find video resources on this topic at:
- www.thinkingseries.com

Chapter Three

Do All Religions Lead to God?

Key Points:

No religion leads to God. God is too great to be reached through our own efforts. Therefore, Christianity teaches that God reached us, through Jesus, for the purpose of relationship.

Key Questions:

1. Where have you traveled? How have your travels affected your view of the world?

2. Is it possible to have a religion that makes no exclusive truth claims at all? What would it look like?

3. What do you think about the idea that all religions are climbing the same mountain? What problems arise from claiming that all religions are true?

4. People in our culture often say, "This is true for me." What do you think about this statement? Is religious truth subjective or objective?

5. Given Andy's summary of the major worldviews, how do you think Hinduism, Buddhism, Islam, and Scientism would answer the question: What's the meaning of life?

6. What was Jesus' worldview? Why should we care how he viewed the world?

7. Read John 8:58-59. What is Jesus saying? Why do the Jews respond that way?

8. Read John 14:1-14. What is Jesus saying about himself and about reaching God? How does this passage support Jesus' teaching on the meaning of life from chapter one?

Key Scriptures:
- Deuteronomy 4:35-40
- Mark 2: 1-12; 14:53-63
- John 1:1; 8:58,59; 14:1-14
- Acts 17:16-34
- Romans 1:20-25

Key Resources:

Easy read:
- *But Don't All Religions Lead to God?* by Michael Green
- *The Illustrated Guide To World Religions* by Dean Halverson

Challenging read:
- *Relativism* by Greg Koukl & Francis Beckwith;
- *Jesus Among Other Gods* by Ravi Zacharias;

Deep read:
- *Philosophical Foundations for a Christian Worldview* by William Lane Craig & J.P. Moreland

Find video resources on this topic at:
- www.thinkingseries.com

Chapter Four

Why is There Evil?

Key Points:

Good can exist without evil because evil is the corruption of good. However, evil cannot exist unless good first exists. Goodness comes from God. God did not create evil; people and angels are responsible for counterfeit good. Although we don't know why God allows evil, free will is a possible answer, especially if God's purpose is real relationships. What we do know is that God loves us and Jesus entered into our suffering to rescue us.

Key Questions:

1. Why do you think people come to different conclusions about God's existence because of suffering and evil? How has evil affected your view of God?

2. Are human beings basically good, morally neutral, or innately depraved? What examples can you provide to defend your view?

3. Read Romans 2:13-15. What is the Apostle Paul saying in this passage? How does this apply to the Nuremberg trials discussed in this chapter?

4. Why would a good God allow people to go to hell? Does God have an alternative?

5. How does Jesus' teaching on the meaning of life from chapter one make sense of the Free Will Defense?

6. Read 2 Corinthians 4:16-18. In light of the existence of evil, in what ways does this passage encourage you, or not?

7. Why is it so difficult for us to trust that God is good and that he will do good?

8. When you experience evil and suffering, what difference does it make to know that Jesus suffered?

Key Scriptures:
- Genesis 3
- Matthew 13:40-42
- John 3:15-16
- Romans 1:20; 2:14-15; 5:12
- 2 Corinthians 4:16-18

Key Resources:
Easy read:
- *The Tears of My Soul* by Sokreaksa Himm;
- *Shantung Compound* by Langdon Gilkey

Challenging read:
- *The Problem of Pain* by C.S. Lewis;
- *Good God* by David Baggett & Jerry Walls

Deep read:
- *The Many Faces of Evil* by John Feinberg

Find video resources on this topic at:
- www.thinkingseries.com

Chapter Five

Is There Life After Death?

Key Points:

Evil brought death into the world. Death separates us from God and from each other. Because Jesus defeated evil and death, we know that Jesus is who he claimed to be. We have hope that there is eternal life—relationship with God after death.

Key Questions:

1. What do you think happens after we die?

2. Andy makes the point that the pain of death is really the pain of relational loss and that our desire for life after death is really a desire for eternal relationship. In what ways is this true or not true for you?

3. What is the difference between a near-death experience and the resurrection of Jesus?

4. The Bible was written over a long time, by many different people, and copied countless times. That being the case, what reasons do you have to trust the historical accuracy of the Bible?

5. Why is understanding the worldview of the disciples important for appreciating the plausibility of the resurrection? Does the resurrection story sound like something that the disciples would have made up?

6. What do you think is the most persuasive evidence that Jesus arose from the dead? Are there any other explanations that better account for all of the evidence?

7. Read 1 Corinthians 15:1-19. Why are the life, death, and resurrection of Jesus so important to the Christian understanding of salvation?

8. Discuss the difference between justice, mercy, and grace. How does the death and resurrection of Jesus exhibit all three of these characteristics perfectly?

Key Scriptures:
- Psalm 16
- Isaiah 53
- Mark 8:27-38
- John 21
- Acts 2:14-36; 17:29-31
- 1 Corinthians 15:1-19

Key Resources:
Easy read:
- *The Case for Christ* by Lee Strobel;
- *Cold Case Christianity* by J. Warner Wallace

Challenging read:
- *The Case for the Resurrection of Jesus* by Gary R. Habermas and Michael R. Licona;
- *The Risen Jesus and Future Hope* by Gary R. Habermas

Deep read:
- *The Resurrection of the Son of God* by N.T. Wright;

Find video resources on this topic at:
- www.thinkingseries.com

Chapter Six

Becoming a Student

Key Points:

If you truly love God, you will love what God loves. God loves people. Therefore, students of Jesus love God and other people. Students of Jesus need to both receive God's grace and extend it towards others.

Key Questions:

1. Do you relate more with Andy's story or with Chris' story? In what ways?

2. Read 1 John 3:16. What are some practical ways that we can lay down our lives for those in need?

3. Read Luke 10:25-37. How do you relate to the story of the Good Samaritan? If you placed yourself in the story, which character would you be, and why?

4. Why is grace so difficult both to receive and to give?

5. How do you define church? What should the role of the church be in a Christian's life and in the world?

6. In what ways does church relate to Jesus' teaching on the meaning of life from chapter one?

7. Have you had someone that mentored you? How did it impact you? Are you mentoring anyone?

8. What has God been teaching you through this book?

Key Scriptures:
- Matthew 28:19-20
- Luke 10:25-37
- 1 Corinthians 11:1
- Ephesians 3:14-21
- 1 John 3:16

Key Resources:

Easy read:
- *Multiply* by Francis Chan;
- *Radical* by David Platt

Challenging read:
- *The Divine Conspiracy* by Dallas Willard;
- *Love Your God With All Your Mind* by J.P. Moreland

Deep read:
- *Following the Master* by Michael J. Wilkinson

Find video resources on this topic at:
- www.thinkingseries.com

About the Coauthor

Sheri Hiebert is an English Literature graduate with a passion for the written word. She strives to use her talent for writing clearly and engagingly to serve God and impact people. Sheri lives in Chilliwack, BC, Canada with her husband DJ and their two children, Hudson and Rosalyn.

THINKING?